IMPORTANT:

HERE IS YOUR REGISTRATION CODE TO ACCESS
YOUR PREMIUM McGRAW-HILL ONLINE RESOURCES.

MCGRAW-HILL

ONLINE RESOURCES

For key premium online resources you need THIS CODE to gain access. Once the code is entered, you will be able to use the Web resources for the length of your course.

If your course is using **WebCT** or **Blackboard**, you'll be able to use this code to access the McGraw-Hill content within your instructor's online course.

Access is provided if you have purchased a new book. If the registration code is missing from this book, the registration screen on our Website, and within your WebCT or Blackboard course, will tell you how to obtain your new code.

Registering for McGraw-Hill Online Resources

TO gain access to your MCGraw-Hill web resources simply follow the steps below:

 (1) USE YOUR WEB BROWSER TO GO TO: **http://register.dushkin.com**

(2) CLICK ON **FIRST TIME USER**.

(3) ENTER THE REGISTRATION CODE* PRINTED ON THE TEAR-OFF BOOKMARK ON THE RIGHT.

(4) AFTER YOU HAVE ENTERED YOUR REGISTRATION CODE, CLICK **REGISTER**.

(5) FOLLOW THE INSTRUCTIONS TO SET-UP YOUR PERSONAL UserID AND PASSWORD

(6) WRITE YOUR UserID AND PASSWORD DOWN FOR FUTURE REFERENCE.
KEEP IT IN A SAFE PLACE.

TO GAIN ACCESS to the McGraw-Hill content in your instructor's **WebCT** or **Blackboard** course simply log in to the course with the UserID and Password provided by your instructor. Enter the registration code exactly as it appears in the box to the right when prompted by the system. You will only need to use the code the first time you click on McGraw-Hill content.

THank you, and welcome to your MCGraw-Hill online Resources!

REGISTRATION CODE

u35ra-eb6p-ai4e-g49g

D1364782

Mc Graw Hill Higher Education

* YOUR REGISTRATION CODE CAN BE USED ONLY ONCE TO ESTABLISH ACCESS. IT IS NOT TRANSFERABLE.
0-07-301690-X T/A KESSLER, SHINTO WAYS OF BEING RELIGIOUS

SHINTO WAYS OF BEING RELIGIOUS

SHINTO WAYS OF BEING RELIGIOUS

Gary E. Kessler
California State University, Bakersfield

Boston   Burr Ridge, IL   Dubuque, IA   Madison, WI   New York   San Francisco   St. Louis
Bangkok   Bogotá   Caracas   Kuala Lumpur   Lisbon   London   Madrid   Mexico City
Milan   Montreal   New Delhi   Santiago   Seoul   Singapore   Sydney   Taipei   Toronto

The McGraw·Hill Companies

Shinto Ways of Being Religious

Published by McGraw-Hill, a business unit of The McGraw-Hill Companies, Inc., 1221 Avenue of the Americas, New York, NY 10020. Copyright © 2005 by The McGraw-Hill Companies, Inc. All rights reserved. No part of this publication may be reproduced or distributed in any form or by any means, or stored in a database or retrieval system, without the prior written consent of The McGraw-Hill Companies, Inc., including, but not limited to, any network or other electronic storage or transmission, or broadcast for distance learning.

Some ancillaries, including electronic and print components, may not be available to customers outside the United States.

This book is printed on acid-free paper.

1 2 3 4 5 6 7 8 9 0 FGR/FGR 0 9 8 7 6 5 4

ISBN 0-07-301689-6

Editor-in-chief and publisher: *Emily Barrosse*
Sponsoring editor: *Jon-David Hague*
Editorial assistant: *Allison Rona*
Senior marketing manager: *Zina Craft*
Permissions editor: *Marty Granahan*
Project manager: *Leslie LaDow*
Lead production supervisor: *Randy Hurst*
Senior designer: *Kim Menning*
Typeface: *9/11 Janson*
Compositor: *Interactive Composition Corporation*
Printer: *Quebecor World Fairfield*

Cover photo: © Digital Stock/CORBIS

Library of Congress Cataloging-in-Publication Data

Kessler, Gary E.
    Shinto Ways of Being Religious / by Gary E. Kessler.
        p.   cm.
    ISBN 0-07-301689-6 (pbk.: alk. paper)
    1. Shinto. I. Title.

BL2220. K427   2004
299.5'61—dc22

To Nature

Contents

Preface

Although Shinto is by no means a "world religion" (having perhaps no more than four million practicing members worldwide), its study is important if for no other reason than the fact that Japan and Japanese culture have had such a widespread influence on so many different cultures, including those of Europe and North America. From business to art, from food to martial arts, all things Japanese have fascinated people from other lands. Any well-educated person should know something about the history and culture of Japan. Learning about Shinto contributes one small part to a person's knowledge of the world. Such knowledge is necessary for a generation that will increasingly experience the effects of globalization.

In addition, the reverence for nature that is deeply embedded in Shinto's worldview provides valuable lessons for us as we face the increasing threat of environmental and ecological disasters.

This collection of sources along with the introductions and reading questions is intended to supplement *Ways of Being Religious* (2000) and *Eastern Ways of Being Religious* (2000). It provides an opportunity for instructors to expand their coverage of East Asian religious traditions with information about Shinto, "the way of the kami."

Gary E. Kessler
March 9, 2004

Introduction

What is Shinto? The usual answer is that Shinto is the indigenous or homegrown religion of Japan. However, in recent years, some scholars have raised doubts about that answer. The word *Shinto* only came into existence after Buddhism was brought to Japan from Korea in the year 538. Prior to that time, there was no name for the religious practices of the Japanese because there was no need to distinguish them from other competing religious practices with distinct names. Further, good evidence exists to conclude that the word *Shinto*, as used in early writing, did not designate a distinct and independent set of religious practices (see Chapter 8). It was not until the nineteenth century that the idea of Shinto as the traditional and native religion of the Japanese became widespread. The idea served political ends because it helped to support the growing nationalism of the rulers of Japan.

Is Shinto a religion? People typically believe that it is indeed a religion. However, it is unlike other religions in significant ways. For example, it has no founder, no scriptures, no systematic ethics, and little concern for otherworldly salvation. Many Japanese do not think of it as a religion in the same way they think of Buddhism or Christianity as religions. For many Japanese Shinto is just part of Japanese culture, much like Americans think of hot dogs, fireworks, and the Fourth of July as part of American culture

rather than elements of a religious festival commemorating the sacred beginnings of the nation. Nevertheless, there are Shinto priests and shrines, and the central focus of many Shinto rituals are the **kami,** a term which some scholars translate as *gods* or *spirits*. Thus, Shinto is like what we commonly call religion in some respects and not in other respects.

You will have occasion, as you read this chapter, to consider these two questions: What is Shinto and is it a religion? Each time you return to these questions it will be with greater understanding of both the wonderful complexity and simplicity of Shinto. Concerns about problems of definition should not prevent your seeing the beauty in Shinto's appreciation of life. Sokyo Ono, a professor at Japan's only Shinto university, concludes his book *Shinto: The Kami Way* with these words:

> People of all races and climes cannot help but express gratitude to the spirits of the land and of nature, to their ancestors, to the benefactors of society and the state. In so far as they recognize this feeling within them, they cannot but understand the spirit of Shinto . . .*

---

*Sokyo Ono, *Shinto: The Kami Way* (Rutland, VT and Tokyo, Japan: Charles E. Tuttle Company, 1962), 111–112.

An Overview

One common way to study a particular religion is the historical approach: If we can understand the development of a religion, we can see how it changes in response to new situations. Its creativity and vitality become evident as we understand the many ways in which a religion reinvents itself in response to change and at the same time seeks to preserve a sense of permanence. This permanence gives people meaning and purpose.

When using an historical approach, we must remind ourselves that dividing time into different periods reflects the views of scholars about what is important and what is not important. Time does not come neatly divided into named periods. Historians divide time and name periods. It has become customary for those who study Japanese history to divide it into different periods. These divisions are scholarly constructions intended to provide useful ways of organizing textual, archeological, artistic, and other cultural products.

Ian Markham, Professor of Theology and Public Life at Liverpool Hope University College, provides in the following selection both an historical overview of Shinto in six time periods and a discussion of some of its key elements. Markham endorses the notion that Shintoism is the indigenous religion of Japan and treats its development as continuous with the practices and beliefs that arose in Japan many centuries ago.

IAN MARKHAM

Shintoism

READING QUESTIONS

1. What are the different meanings of the term *kami?*
2. What are the important differences between the early period and the Heian period?
3. What are the three different layers of Japanese society that developed in the Tokugawa period, and how did Shinto operate differently in each layer?
4. What was the impact of the Meiji Restoration on Shinto?
5. Why did State Shinto come to an end after World War II?
6. How does the information the author provides about worldview, institutions, rituals, festivals, ethics, and women support his claims that gratitude, appreciation of natural beauty, and concerns with ritual purity are at the heart of Shinto?
7. With what unanswered questions about Shinto does this overview leave you?

From Ian Markham, "Shintoism," *Encountering Religion: An Introduction to the Religions of the World*, 296–307. Copyright © Blackwell Publishers, Ltd. 2001. Editorial matter and arrangement copyright © Ian S. Markham and Tinu Ruparell, 2001. Reprinted by permission of Blackwell Publishers.

Winston Davies, a leading authority on Shintoism, walked into a tea shop in Tokyo just before it officially opened:

> As I sat waiting, the employees joined hands and chanted the following credo:
> We are grateful to the people of the world.
> We will not forget that our shop has been set up for the sake of the customer.
> Sharing both happiness and sorrow, we will cooperate and not forget to encourage each other.
> Setting aside the past and anxiety of the 'morrow we will not forget to give our all to the work set before us today![1]

The credo begins with a sense of gratitude. This sense of gratitude is, perhaps, the key to understanding Shintoism. One is grateful to one's parents—for life, food, clothing—and grateful to village gods and one's ancestors—for land, possessions, and employment. It is this sense of "givenness" that generates the famous sense of Japanese obligation.

As with most religions, generalizations are difficult. It is often said that Shintoism represents the values and dispositions of Japanese culture. Although this is true to an extent, it is important to remember that most nations are made up of many cultures . . . [and that] Shintoism embraces considerable diversity. In particular it is not at all clear where Shintoism ends and Buddhism starts. This is partly due to the lack of organization. As we shall see, one had to wait until 1900 for a comprehensive, national organization. Yet it is right to describe Shintoism as the indigenous religion of Japan, which for centuries did not need a name. The name "Shinto" (taken from *shen do (dao, tao)*) arose in the sixth century CE precisely to distinguish itself from Buddhism. As Buddhism was the "Way of the Buddha" so Shintoism described itself as the old way, "The Way of the Gods" or a better translation "The Way of the Kami." Kami is a difficult term to describe. In brief, kami are the forces and powers that pervade everything; they are seen best in "extraordinary" things of life—the sun, thunder, great people (such as Emperors) and animals. As this idea is very important, more shall be said about the kami later on.

Shintoism distinguishes itself from the other faith traditions in a number of ways. Although it has books that are revered, it does not really have a scripture. Although it does make ethical demands, it does not really have a strong code of ethical behavior. It is also extremely significant historically. After World War II, the postwar surrender treaty built in a requirement that the Shinto religion must be disestablished. This chapter will explore all these elements. However, to begin with we shall start with a brief historical survey, which will be followed by a systematic account of Shintoism.

SHINTOISM IN THE PAST

THE EARLY PERIOD

The first Japanese histories were written down in the eighth century BCE. Prior to this, we have a small number of clues. There are Chinese documents from the third century, which describe visits of people to Japan, and a significant archeological record. Everything seems to suggest that the Japanese had a strong appreciation of the beauty of the natural world. They loved their island home. The power of nature and the miracle of fertility preoccupied them greatly. They wanted to merge with nature rather than fight or resist it. Anything provoking awe, either in nature, amongst people, or beyond, provoked worship. This is where the idea of kami comes from. In early Japanese history, considerable prominence is given to the story of the descent of the Imperial family from the supreme Sun Goddess.

It also seems that from the "start" (whenever that was) government and religion were closely linked together. Sacred leaders, who in early times were female shamans, were responsible both for organizing the worship of the kami and for the organization of human affairs. There was no clear philosophy or ethics. Instead the focus was a sense of gratitude and joy for life and a real intimacy with nature. This intimacy partly depended on "ritual purity." One had to be clean to be close to the kami. The theme of purity has continued to be a major part of Shintoism right up to the present day.

A link between the political and religious realms can be found in the very earliest Japanese clans. The government of eighth-century Japan saw it as their responsibility to organize the major religious festivals and to maintain the shrines. The Emperor's function combined administrative duties with his religious ones. The stability of the cosmic order depended on this combination. It is not surprising that it was during this period that the two major texts of Shintoism were written. *Kojiki* was written in 712 and *Nihongi* in 720. These two texts outline two central themes of Shintoism: the existence of kami throughout Japan and the "semi-divine" descent of Japan and her people.

PERIOD 2: HEIAN PERIOD

Shintoism has shown itself remarkable in its capacity to assimilate different influences. Two centuries before the Heian period (794–1185), the sophisticated Chinese had arrived. The Japanese welcomed the highly developed and complex system of Confucian political life. They worked hard to impose order on their informal tribal systems. Although the Chinese political system dissipated over time, the Confucian ethic became a significant part of Japanese life that continues to this very day. However, in the Heian period, Buddhism emerged as a major influence. Although Buddhism had already arrived and taken root with Nara Buddhism, the Heian period saw the emergence of two further Buddhist sects. As in many other countries in Asia, Buddhists were good at accommodating local religions. A popular Buddhist strategy was to suggest that the local deities were simply the local expression of Buddhist experience. So, for example, the Buddhist monks of the Shingon sect described the local kami as expressions of bodhisattvas (enlightened beings). Kobo Daishi was the founder of Shingon: he introduced a highly esoteric Buddhism that had its roots in the Tantric traditions of India. The second sect emerging in this period was the Tendai, founded by Dengyo Daishi. The famous Chinese text the *Lotus Sutra* was its central scripture and its Japanese headquarters was the Hieizan mountain. It was also during this period that Taoism became important. Japanese religion was a hybrid of Shintoism, Buddhism, and religious Taoism, which took distinctive Japanese expression. Shugendo, for example, was a highly organized pilgrimage movement of this period: it stressed the need to make pilgrimage to sacred mountains and acknowledge the power of the local kami on these mountains, which were linked to the local bodhisattvas of Buddhism. Shintoism was now inescapably linked with other religious traditions. Scholars disagree as to the extent of this linkage. Helen Hardacre insists that the practice of Shinto was for centuries a "mere appendage to Buddhist institutions."[2] Brian Bocking insists that "For most of its history what we call in retrospect Shinto was mainly Buddhism, with generous helpings of Taoism, Yin–Yang philosophy, Confucianism, folk religion and more recently European-style nationalism."[3] Edwin O. Reischauer is more nuanced and more accurate when he writes, "[T]he two religions became institutionally very much intertwined. . . . And

yet, throughout, Shinto retained its distinctiveness and strength."[4] Although it is true that we have to wait until 1900 for the basics of a national Shinto organization, it is wrong to deny the existence of distinctive Shinto beliefs and dispositions before this. It is true, however, that Buddhism and Shintoism were both operating together in Japanese culture up until 1868.

PERIOD 3: KAMAKURA PERIOD

The Heian period was marked by political and social stability. The Kamakura period (1185–1333) was much more troubled. Political power shifted from the Court to the shoguns (the feudal powers). Struggles between these feudal powers, which had their roots in the Heian period, now dominated the political scene. Religiously, many of the syncretistic tendencies of the Heian period continued. However, as is common in troubled times, a widespread belief arose that the people were living in the third and final age of the world. (The first age was a period when people practiced the Buddha's teaching and obtained enlightenment; the second was a period of practice but few expected to obtain enlightenment; and the third was a period of indifference to the teaching and virtually no observation.) Given that this was the final age, an expectation developed that the world would end soon, probably through a great catastrophe. The forms of Buddhism that emerged in this period reflected these expectations. It is not surprising that the Pure Land Sects and the Zen Sects emerged during this period.

PERIOD 4: TOKUGAWA PERIOD

Perhaps partly in reaction to the unsettled nature of the preceding period, the Tokugawa period was marked by strong central government, peace, and order. Its attitude to religion was strongly conservative. Helen Hardacre suggests that Shintoism in the period operated differently within the three different layers of Japanese society. The first layer was the "ritual practice of the imperial court, which maintained a formal schedule of elaborate ritual for both Buddhas and kami."[5] It was during this period that the widespread Japanese practice of Shinto ritual to mark birth and Buddhist ritual to mark death became a commonplace. The second layer consisted of the large shrines that had sufficient resources to support an hereditary priesthood. Many were branch shrines (i.e., linked with an original shrine through a ceremony); often these shrines were a result of the migration of members from the original shrine and as they settled so they created a new shrine dedicated to the clan deity. Many of the most prestigious shrines, such as Usa Hachiman, Inari, Kasuga, Tenjin, Konpira, Munakata, Suwa, and Izumo, developed branch shrines throughout Japan. The third layer involved the many thousands of local shrines dedicated to a local tutelary deity. Often these shrines did not have a professional priest, but simply survived through the support of the local community.

Toward the end of the Tokugawa period, two distinct developments emerged. The Ise pilgrimage was the means by which many Japanese people found themselves involved in the worship of kami. Villages would support certain carefully chosen pilgrims as they traveled to the shrine to offer prayers for a bounteous harvest. The second development was the Shinto school of thought known as National Learning. This school has its roots in the work of Kada no Azumamaro (1669–1739), but in the nineteenth century was heavily shaped by Hirata Atsutane (1776–1843). The key issues for this school were the separation of Shinto from Buddhism, the need for Shinto funerals taken by a Shinto priest, and the reestablishment of a department of religion within the government.

PERIOD 5: THE MEIJI RESTORATION

Tokugawa feudalism came to an end with the Meiji Restoration (1868). Earhart sees this date as the movement of Japan into the modern world. Although ostensibly the restoration is so called because the Emperor was restored to his position as head of state, in fact it was the period when a modern nation state was formed. Earhart outlines the extent of the change, when he writes: "The whole system of government was reorganized along the lines of a nation-state. The office of the military ruler was abolished and the emperor formally ruled a centralized government with a constitution and elected legislators. The feudal clans were replaced with prefectures which administered local government as a branch of the central authority. The new capital was established at Tokyo. To finance the government a tax system was adopted."[6]

On the religious front, it was the period when the state started to support Shinto as the state religion. A campaign was waged against Buddhism. In the same way that the Emperor had been "restored" so, the argument went, the original religion of Japan had to be "restored." This meant the removal of Buddhist statues and Buddhist priests from Shinto shrines.

During the 1870s, the government found it difficult to insist on Shintoism as the main and most important religion in Japan. Japanese Buddhism was not going to be so easily dismissed. Between 1872 and 1875 the government had a Department of Religion which included both Shintoism and Buddhism. Matters were finally resolved in 1882, when the government formally recognized State Shintoism. Legally State Shintoism was not religious; it was simply the values and institutions that supported the State. Sect Shintoism was a religion (i.e., the 13 groups which were linked with Shintoism) and this was distinct from State Shintoism. The government argued that religion was separate from the State, thereby protecting religious liberty.

Although religious diversity was permitted in Japan, Shinto dominated the scene right up until 1945. After the 1890s, every child in Japan was given a complete introduction to Shinto and a strongly nationalistic ethic (see Markham, *A World Religions Reader*, pp. 203–5). It is a widespread perception that Shinto is responsible for Japan's military aggression. Actually most religious traditions in Japan supported Japan's war activities. Although it is true that the State used Shinto to encourage a patriotic and nationalistic outlook, it would be wrong to simply link the Japanese war machine to the Shinto religion.

PERIOD 6: AFTER WORLD WAR II

The surrender and occupation of Japan in 1945 brought State Shintoism to an end. William K. Brunce headed up the Religions Division of the Civil Information and Education Section and produced the Shinto Directive on December 15, 1945. This directive prohibited the funding of Shinto doctrines and the supporting of any ideology that encouraged militarism and ultranationalism. It also prohibited any creed asserting the superiority of the Emperor or the Japanese people. The Emperor duly announced that he was only human and not a god. The occupying powers were insisting that Shintoism should be treated just like Buddhism and Christianity. Shinto priests no longer worked for the State; Shinto shrines did not receive a state subsidy; and religious nationalistic sentiments were removed from the school textbooks.

The result was a crisis within Shintoism. Its popularity waned rapidly; it was a religion directly associated with the defeat. Once isolated from government it found itself lacking sufficient organization, which hampered the tradition's capacity to recover. For many years it looked as if Shintoism was in serious trouble. However, in recent years it has recovered, or perhaps, to be more accurate, it has demonstrated how it has remained part of the Japanese psyche.

This perhaps can be best illustrated by the controversy surrounding the death of Emperor Hirohito who died on January 7, 1989. The Crown Prince Akihito succeeded him on January 8, 1989, but the enthronement ceremony was not held until November 1990. During the intervening period, the whole issue of state funding for the enthronement had to be confronted.

Article 89 of the Constitution of Japan (1946) states explicitly: "no public money or other property shall be expended . . . for the use, benefit or maintenance of any religious institution or association . . ." This article would appear to prohibit funding for either the funeral or the enthronement. However, the strength of the "traditionalists" (i.e., those who insisted that Japanese traditions must be maintained) was sufficient for the government to be persuaded to pay for these rituals. For the funeral, the government divided the occasion into a "religious private ceremony" and a "secular public part," both of which were paid for out of the public purse. For the enthronement, the government made a similiar distinction. The actual enthronement ceremony (Sokui-no-Rei) was considered a state affair and paid for out of state funds. The Daijosai ceremony, which is the occasion when the Emperor assumes spiritual power by spending part of a night in a special Shinto shrine, was to be funded out of the Imperial court budget. The court budget comes from the government, so it is a moot point whether this careful distinction made any difference.

There are some movements that would like the government to extend further funding to certain other shrines. Such movements are vigorously opposed, especially by Christians, who fear a repeat of the 1930s. The result is that Shintoism continues to gain widespread recognition, although the government tries to keep its distance.

SHINTOISM TODAY

WORLDVIEWS

Kami

The concept of kami probably has its roots in the Japanese love of nature. According to tradition there are many thousands (*yaoyorozu no kami*—vast myriads of kami) of these life powers. Although the Sun Kami Amaterasu-o-Mikami is considered the head of the kami, she is not considered the source or the overall creator. Indeed she pays respect to the other kami. This means that unlike many other traditions there is a fundamental plurality of forces in control of the world.

The central texts that describe the main kami are the Kojiki and Nihongi. It is here that the marvelous Japanese story of the creator is recorded; the emergence of the Japanese islands from the love of two creator kami—Izanagi and Izanami. Kami are found throughout nature: mountains, trees, rocks, sea, rivers, and animals. Even people can be described as kami, not least the Emperor. Naturally there are those kami which are destructive and cause suffering, for example Magatsuhi-no-kami (the kami of misfortune). Traditionally such destructive kami are located in the netherworld (the land of Yomi). Evil, in Shintoism, is not inherent in humanity but comes from outside.

The primary human duty toward the kami is to worship them. All deserve respect, even the destructive kami. There are thousands of shrines in Japan. All insist on approaching the kami having observed the fundamental rituals of purification. Then it is possible to offer food, offer dances and music, and chant prayers. Some homes have a kami shelf (*kamidana*). This is a miniature shrine, which is often decorated with pine sprigs or the sacred *sasaki* tree. The family will deposit various offerings on the shelf (e.g., rice cakes or seaweed) and demonstrate their acknowledgment of the kami by clapping, bowing, and praying in front of the shrine.

The concept of kami is a distinctive Japanese contribution to the understanding of the spiritual in the world. Only certain forms of Hinduism and animism are similiar. It is the acknowledgment of the many varied powers that maintain the balance of the cosmos. The worship of the kami is essential to maintain the harmony of the human with nature.

Kojiki (Records of Ancient Matters) and Nihongi (Chronicles of Japan)

These are the earliest texts of Shintoism. Emperor Temmu (672–86) felt that existing histories were unreliable and offered to provide a corrected text. The Kojiki was compiled first in 712 CE, closely followed by the Nihongi, which according to tradition was compiled in 720 CE. The major theme of the Kojiki is the origin of kingship. Book 1 explains the origins of the world through the marriage of two kami, Izanagi and Izanami. Together they create the Japanese islands and many other kami. Izanami is then killed by the kami of fire, so Izanagi descends to the underworld to try and find her. When Izanagi returns to the earth, the act of purification brings about the existence of the Kami of the Sun, Amaterasu. She is the historic ancestor of the Imperial family. She is the administrator of the heavenly domain. It is her grandson Ninigi who descends from heaven to Mount Takachiho to rule the Japanese islands.

Book 2 starts with the great-grandson of Ninigi, Jimmu, who becomes Japan's first Emperor. Jimmu goes to war against the forces of evil and finds the center of the land, which is where he builds the Imperial Palace. We are then provided with a careful record of 13 other Emperors before arriving at Emperor Ojin, who historians have evidence lived in the fifth century CE. Book 3 continues to document the achievements of the great Emperors. It describes their exploits, from Emperor Nintoku to Empress Suiko.

Nihongi covers similiar ground. There are thirty volumes, of which the first two deal with the age of the kami and the remaining twenty-eight tell the story from Emperor Jimmu to Empress Jito. It seems that the two books are intended for different audiences. The Nihongi has made use of more sources; it seems to be intended as an official chronicle, comparable to the historical records of the Chinese.

INSTITUTIONS AND RITUALS

The Shrine Association (Jinja Honcho)

On February 3, 1946, the Shrine Association was formed. This is the body responsible for coordinating and governing "shrine Shinto." After the breakdown of "State Shintoism," this was the body that emerged to coordinate continuing Shinto activities. Although some shrines are independent of the Association, more than 80 percent of Japanese shrines are affiliated to it. Relatively recently the headquarters were moved from Tokyo to Meiji jingu. The central teaching is the "guidance of the spiritual leadership of the Ise shrines" because this embodies the spiritual homeland of Japan. The Ise Shrine is the Imperial household shrine, which is identified with the Emperor; it remains popular as a place of pilgrimage. The Association retains certain traditional convictions about the character of Shinto: for example, it assumes the Shinto is a national faith, which is separate from Buddhism. The president is responsible for the recognition of priestly rank and the appointment of priests to shrines. On certain other occasions the president stands in for the Emperor.

FESTIVALS

The Shinto word which is closest to "festivals" is matsuri. According to Brian Bocking, this term may be rendered "festival," "worship," "celebration," "rite," or even "prayer," which actually captures the range of activities connected with Shinto festivals.[7] The main Shinto festivals are organized around the annual seasonal celebrations. Most are held at a shrine and will involve offering, prayers, rites, gratitude to the kami, and straightforward entertainment.

MAJOR FESTIVALS

Oshogatsu (New Year)	1–3 January
Ohinamatsuri (Dolls' or Girls' Festival)	3 March
Tango nu Sekku (Boys' Festival)	5 May
Hoshi matsuri/Tanabata (Star Festival)	7 July

Ethics

Shintoism is not preoccupied with "ethics." Bocking explains that Japanese do not associate the Shinto word shushin with morality and behavioral norms, but with "the pre-war ethics courses and textbooks used in Japanese schools to underpin the emperor system."[8] For Bocking, the ethics of Shinto are simply Japanese versions of Confucianism or Buddhism.

Insofar that Shintoism has an ethic, it is one that stresses the corporate dimensions of human life. Sokyo Ono writes, "The Shinto faith brings not only the individual, the neighbourhood and society into direct relationship with the kami and makes them more ideal; it does the same for the political world."[9] As we saw in the examination of the history of Shintoism, it is true that Shintoism has been a bond that linked the people with nature and the state. This, of course, partly created the problems that led to the Allies requiring the disestablishment of State Shinto at the end of World War II. Sokyo Ono insists that the use of Shinto for nationalistic purposes was a distortion of the tradition and writes, "[F]undamentally, Shinto is a faith which is based on the belief that many kami cooperate together. Shrine Shinto is worship to unite and harmonize the various kinds of kami. The spirit of tolerance and cooperation is a hitherto unnoticed aspect of Shinto."[10] Generally, however, there is little that is distinctive about Shinto ethics. Japanese ethical traditions do not draw heavily on the Shinto tradition.

Women

Some feminist scholars suspect that Shintoism historically was positive about women.[11] There is some evidence that prior to the sixth century CE there was a female shamanic cult and that menstruating women were viewed positively as possessed by kami and pure. Problems arose with the arrival of the more male-dominated Buddhist traditions, which marginalized Shinto shamanesses and, perhaps, women more generally. However, as Martinez has shown, the domination of the major festivals by men can easily lead scholars to ignore the way that women dominate the minor rituals and festivals.

Martinez provides a study of a Kuzaki village. She shows how the bulk of household rites are organized by women. The daily offerings to the kami and the prayers to household ancestors are almost always performed by the women. Even the monthly climb up Sengen, the sacred mountain, is an activity of the working women. This monthly pilgrimage is to ask the kami for good fortune. It was only when the village celebrated a major festival that the men became involved. All the political leaders were present, all of whom were men, and they dominated the occasion.

For Martinez, the interesting feature is the way that the regular acts of rituals are being dominated by women. She suggests that "women, . . . because of their innate power, always have the potential to mediate directly for the deities."[12] In other words there is a constructive message underpinning this, largely rural, participation in religious activities.

Modern Expression

It is commonplace that western scholars of Japanese religions find themselves denying the existence of Japanese religion. The education system stresses the worlds of technology and science and is impatient with the "spiritual." Book shops are full of books on ghosts, avoiding pollution, and UFOs. Ian Reader insists that there is considerable evidence that Japanese young people are reacting against such reductionism. He writes, "The processes of modernisation, rationalisation, scientific development and increased education thus tend to stimulate rather than diminish interest in spiritual matters and the world of the irrational."[13] Religion is alive and well in Japan.

Yet traditional forms are struggling. The evidence is that it is anti-establishment traditions that attract the interest. Shintoism continues to be identified with the "establishment." However, Ian Reader writes, "the rising numbers participating in festivals, . . . the various occasions which memorialize the ancestors, the current interest in pilgrimages, the large numbers who acquire amulets and talismans and visit religious centers to pray for benefits, the small but growing interest in meditation . . . , the contemporary focus on ascetic and charismatic figures of power, and the seemingly endless emergence and growth of new religions, are indicative of the energies inherent in the religious world of Japan today."[14]

Shintoism remains significant because underpinning many festivals and customs are Shinto traditions. In the 1980s, growing Japanese prosperity enabled the Japanese to revisit their traditions with pride. In the 1990s, the economic miracle was less strong and interest in religious traditions waned. It seems to remain true that interest in Shintoism runs in parallel with Japanese self-perception; when the Japanese nation is doing well, Shintoism is viewed positively; when it is doing less well, Shintoism attracts less interest.

NOTES AND REFERENCES

1. Winston Davis, *Japanese Religion and Society: Paradigms of Structure and Change* (New York: State University of New York, 1992), pp. 18–19.
2. Helen Hardacre, *Shinto and the State 1868–1988* (Princeton: Princeton University Press, 1989), p. 5. Hardacre makes much of the lack of official organization and follows Kuroda Toshio's argument at this point.
3. Brian Bocking, *A Popular Dictionary of Shinto* (Richmond: Curzon, 1995), p. viii.
4. Edwin O. Reischauer, in Roger Eastman (ed.), *The Ways of Religion* (Oxford: Oxford University Press, 1993), p. 243.
5. Helen Hardacre, *Shinto and the State* (Princeton: Princeton University Press, 1989), p. 10.
6. H. Byron Earhart, *Japanese Religion: Unity and Diversity* (Belmont, California: Dickenson Publishing Co., 1969), p. 76.
7. Brian Bocking, *A Popular Dictionary of Shinto* (Richmond: Curzon, 1995), p. 117.
8. Ibid., p. 186.
9. Sokyo Ono, *Shinto: The Kami Way* (Rutland, Vermont, and Tokyo: Charles E. Tuttle Co., 1962), p. 75.
10. Ibid., p. 79.
11. Much of the material in this section is taken from D. P. Martinez, "Women and ritual," in Jan van Bremen and D. P. Martinez (eds.), *Ceremony and Ritual in Japan* (London and New York: Routledge, 1995), pp. 186ff.
12. Ibid., p. 194.
13. Ian Reader, *Religion in Contemporary Japan* (Basingstoke: Macmillan Press, 1991), p. 236.
14. Ibid., pp. 236–7.

SOURCES

The source material is organized historically, following for the most part the time periods delineated by Markham in the overview. The dates here will vary somewhat from those in the previous selection because the time divisions between periods are only approximations. We begin with what Markham calls the early period.

The Early Period (11,000 B.C.E.?–794)

Humans first migrated from Asia to the eight islands that we today call Japan some 30,000 years ago. Archeological evidence from the Jomon period (from around 11,000 to 300 B.C.E.), the start of the early period, indicates that people at that time were concerned with fertility, death, and the power of the sun. This evidence includes a variety of sacred stones, which appeared to play an important role in the culture. Among these artifacts are stone figurines of women and phalli as well as stone circles. It is difficult, without written records, to know the religious meaning of this archeological evidence, but these artifacts sufficiently resemble what has been found at other Neolithic sites to infer that the early Japanese were concerned with reproduction and the fate of the dead.

2.1 DEATH, POLLUTION, AND QUEEN HIMIKO

The following selection comes from records of the Chinese kingdom of Wei. In these records, we find references to a country called Wa (Japan). These records also tell us that women wore their hair in loops and that men tattooed their bodies. Two passages from these records are particularly interesting, and they follow below. One refers to burial practices and indicates that contact with the dead caused people to become polluted and hence in need of purification. The other refers to a queen and sorceress named Himiko (c. 180–248) who, curiously, is not mentioned in the earliest Japanese records.

History of the Kingdom of Wei (c. 297)

READING QUESTIONS

1. Why do you think that a rite of purification was required after contact with the dead?
2. Assuming the description of Himiko is correct, why do you think she was isolated from the people she ruled?

When a person dies, they prepare a single coffin, without an outer one. They cover the graves with earth to make a mound. When death occurs, mourning is observed for more than ten days, during which period they do not eat meat. The head mourners wail and lament, while friends sing, dance, and drink liquor. When the funeral is over, all members of the family go into the water to cleanse themselves in a bath of purification . . .

The following passages are quoted in Michiko Yusa, *Japanese Religious Traditions* (Upper Saddle River, NJ: Prentice Hall, 2002), 21. See also "Accounts of the Eastern Barbarians: History of the Kingdom of Wei," in *Sources of the Japanese Tradition*, vol. 1, ed. William Theodore De Bary (New York: Columbia University Press, 1958), 4–6.

She [Himiko] occupied herself with magic and sorcery, bewitching the people. Though mature in age, she remained unmarried. She had a younger brother who assisted her in ruling the country. After she became ruler, there were few who saw her. She had one thousand women attendants, but only one man. He served her food and drink and acted as a medium of communication. She resided in a palace surrounded by towers and stockades, with armed guards in a state of constant vigilance.

2.2 CLASSICAL MYTHOLOGY

The *Kojiki* (*Records of Ancient Matters*) written in 712 and the **Nihongi** (*Chronicles of Japan,* also titled *Nihon shoki*) written in 720 are the earliest written Japanese sources. These writings set forth the main themes that people have come to associate with Shintoism: pollution/purification, worship of kami, oneness with nature, aesthetic appreciation, divination, and use of oracles delivered by shamanic mediums. Like so many other myths of origin, the stories of the creation of the Japanese islands and the generations of the kami serve to legitimate and sanctify the right to rule. They tell of the relationship between **Izanagi** ("the male who invites") and **Izanami** ("the female who invites"), of their offspring the Sun Goddess **Amaterasu,** and of the descent of Jimmu, the first emperor, from the kami.

Through these classical writings, we learn much about the kami. The kami bring order out of chaos by partitioning the universe into heaven (over which Amaterasu rules), the sea (over which the wind kami **Susanoo** rules), and the night (over which the moon kami **Tsukiyomi** rules). These are the three "august children" of Izanagi and Izanami. Just as the kami create order on the macrocosmic scale, the imperial household that descends from them brings social order on the microcosmic level. The following selection comes from the classic *Kojiki.*

TRANSLATED BY JOSEPH M. KITAGAWA

Kojiki

READING QUESTIONS

1. How were the islands of Japan created?
2. How would you interpret the story about Izanagi going to Hades to see his wife Izanami? Can you think of any similar stories from other cultures?
3. How would you interpret the story about the retrieval of the Sun Goddess Amaterasu from the cave?
4. What political purpose might the stories about Ninigi and grandson Jimmu serve?

A. MYTHS REGARDING THE PLAIN OF HIGH HEAVEN

1. BIRTH OF KAMI

At the beginning of heaven and earth, there came into existence in the Plain of High Heaven the Heavenly Center Lord Kami, next, the Kami of High Generative Force, and then the Kami of Divine Generative Force.

Next, when the earth was young, not yet solid, there developed something like reed shoots from which the Male Kami of Excellent Reed Shoots and then Heavenly Eternal Standing Kami emerged.

The above five kami are the heavenly kami of special standing. (*Kojiki* [Records of ancient matters], ch. 1)

Then, there came into existence Earth Eternal Standing Kami, Kami of Abundant Clouds Field, male and female Kami of Clay, male and female Kami of Post, male and female Kami of Great Door, Kami of

Complete Surface and his spouse, Kami of Awesomeness, Izanagi (kami-who-invites) and his spouse, Izanami (kami-who-is-invited). (*Ibid.*, ch. 2)

2. SOLIDIFICATION OF THE LAND AND THE DIVINE MARRIAGE

The heavenly kami at this time gave the heavenly jeweled spear to Izanagi and Izanami and instructed them to complete and solidify the land. Thus, the two kami, standing on the floating bridge in Heaven, lowered the spear and stirred around, and as they lifted up the spear, the brine dripping from the tip of the spear piled up and formed an island. This was the island of Onogoro. (*Ibid.*, ch. 3)

Descending from heaven to this island, Izanagi asked his spouse Izanami as to how her body was formed. She replied, "My body is formed in such a way that one spot is not filled." Then Izanagi said, "My body is formed in such a way that there is one spot which is filled in excess. How would it be if I insert the portion of my body which is formed to excess into that portion of your body which is not filled and give birth to the land?" Izanami replied, "That would be excellent." Then Izanagi said, "Let us then walk around the heavenly pillar and meet and have conjugal intercourse." (*Ibid.*, ch. 4)

3. BIRTH OF OTHER KAMI

After giving birth to the land, they proceeded to bear kami [such as the kami of the wind, of the tree, of the mountain, and of the plains]. But Izanami died after giving birth to the kami of fire. (*Ibid.*, ch. 7)

Izanagi, hoping to meet again with his spouse, went after her to the land of Hades. When Izanami came out to greet him, Izanagi said, "Oh my beloved, the land which you and I have been making has not yet been completed. Therefore, you must return with me." To which Izanami replied, "I greatly regret that you did not come here sooner, for I have already partaken of the hearth of the land of hades. But let me discuss with the kami of hades about my desire to return. You must, however, not look at me." As she was gone so long,

Izanagi, being impatient, entered the hall to look for her and found maggots squirming around the body of Izanami. (*Ibid.*, ch. 9)

Izanagi, seeing this, was afraid and ran away, saying, "Since I have been to an extremely horrible and unclean land, I must purify myself." Thus, arriving at [a river], he purified and exorcised himself. When he washed his left eye, there came into existence the Sun Goddess, or Heavenly Illuminating Great Kami (Amaterasu), and when he washed his right eye, there emerged the Moon Kami (Tsukiyomi). Finally, as he washed his nose there came into existence Valiant Male Kami (Susanoo). (*Ibid.*, chs. 10, 11)

Greatly rejoiced over this, Izanagi removed his necklace, and giving it to the Sun Goddess, he gave her the mission to rule the Plain of High Heaven. Next he entrusted to the Moon Kami the rule of the realms of the night. Finally, he gave Valiant Male Kami the mission to rule the ocean. (*Ibid.*, ch. 12)

4. WITHDRAWAL OF THE SUN GODDESS

[At one time] the Sun Goddess [shocked by the misdeeds of her brother, Valiant Male Kami], opened the heavenly rock-cave door and concealed herself inside. Then the Plain of High Heaven became completely dark, and all manner of calamities arose.

Then the 800 myriads of kami gathered in a divine assembly, and summoned Kami of the Little Roof in Heaven and Kami of Grand Bead to perform a divination. They hung long strings of myriad curved beads on the upper branches of a sacred tree, and hung a large-dimensioned mirror on its middle branches. They also suspended in the lower branches white and blue cloth. These objects were held by Kami of Grand Bead as solemn offerings, while Kami of the Little Roof in Heaven intoned liturgical prayers (*norito*). Meanwhile, Kami of Heavenly Strength hid himself behind the entrance of the rock-cave, and Kami of Heavenly Headgear bound her sleeves with a cord of vine, and stamped on an overturned bucket which was placed before the rock-cave. Then she became kami-possessed, exposed her breasts and genitals. Thereupon, the

800 myriads of kami laughed so hard that the Plain of High Heaven shook with their laughter.

The Sun Goddess, intrigued by all this, opened the rock-cave door slightly, wondering why it was that the 800 myriads of kami were laughing. Then Kami of Heavenly Headgear said, "There is a kami nobler than you, and that is why we are happy and dancing." While she was speaking thus, Kami of the Little Roof and Kami of Grand Bead showed the mirror to the Sun Goddess. Thereupon, the Sun Goddess, thinking this ever more strange, gradually came out of the cave, and the hidden Kami of Grand Bead took her hand and pulled her out. Then as the Sun Goddess reappeared, the Plain of High Heaven was naturally illuminated. (*Ibid.*, ch. 17)

5. PACIFICATION OF THE IZUMO REGION

[According to the *Kojiki* myth, the Sun Goddess dispatched two divine messengers to pacify the Central Land of the Reed Plains, which was ruled by Great Land Ruler Kami. The two kami persuaded the sons of Great Land Ruler Kami to surrender, and then approached the ruler himself.]

"Your sons have promised not to disobey the commands of the heavenly kami. What is your sentiment on the matter?" To this question he replied, "In keeping with the words of my sons, I too will not disobey and present this Central Land of the Reed Plains in accordance with your commands. However, I would like to have my dwelling place built modelled after the heavenly dwelling with the posts firmly embedded in the bed-rock below and the cross-beams raised high reaching the Plain of High Heaven. Then, I will retire there, and my children the 180 kami will serve the heavenly kami." As he said these words, he hid himself, and a heavenly temple palace was established for him in the land of Izumo. The grandson of the Kami of the Sea Straights served the food and pronounced the words of blessing. (*Ibid.*, ch. 37)

6. DESCENT OF NINIGI, GRANDSON OF THE SUN GODDESS

[As the pacification of the Japanese islands was duly reported, Ninigi, the grandson of the Sun Goddess, was sent to rule the land with the following instruction.]

"This Land of the Plentiful Reed Plains and of the Fresh Rice-ears has been entrusted to you as the land to be governed by you. Therefore, you must descend from heaven in accordance with the divine command." (*Ibid.*, ch. 38)

Then Ninigi, accompanied by Kami of the Little Roof in Heaven, Kami of Grand Bead, Kami of Heavenly Headgear, Kami of Stone Cutter, and Jewel Ancestor Kami, descended from heaven. The Sun Goddess gave Ninigi the myriad curved beads, the mirror, and the "grass-mower" sword, and also commissioned Thought Collecting Golden Kami of the Eternal World and two other kami to accompany Ninigi. She said, "Take this mirror as my spirit, and venerate it as you would venerate my own presence. Also, let Thought Collecting Golden Kami of the Eternal World take charge of affairs which come before you, and let him carry on the government matters."

Thus, Ninigi, now leaving the heavenly rock seat, pushed through the myriad layers of heavenly clouds and descended on the peak of Mount Takachiho. (*Ibid.*, ch. 39)

B. LEGENDARY HEROES

1. EMPEROR JIMMU (FIRST LEGENDARY EMPEROR)

[Jimmu], living with his brother Lord of Five Rapids in the palace of Takachiho, asked one day, "Where will be the most strategic place for us to live in order to govern the country peacefully? I am inclined to go eastward for that purpose." (*Ibid.*, ch. 47)

As Jimmu thus travelled [eastward] and came to the village of Kumano, he saw a large bear move around and disappear. Suddenly Jimmu as well as his entire army felt faint and lay down. At this time a certain man called Takakuraji appeared with a sword, and as he presented the sword to him, Jimmu suddenly awoke and said, "I must have slept a long time." At the moment when he received that sword, all the unruly kami in the Kumano mountains were slain instantaneously. (*Ibid.*, ch. 49)

Jimmu, after pacifying the unruly kami and the unsubmissive people, dwelled in the palace of Kashiwara at Unebi and ruled the kingdom. (*Ibid.*, ch. 52)

Heian Period (794–1192)

By the dawning of the Heian period, Confucianism, Taoism, and Buddhism had already been influencing Japanese life for several centuries. Confucianism supported the Japanese concern with family and the sacred ancestors. The Japanese became accustomed to thinking of the kami as expressions of Buddhist *bodhisattvas*, and the Taoist sense of the sacredness of nature reinforced Shinto sensibilities. However, the Shinto concern with spirit possession, exorcism, pollution, and purification was still very much a part of everyday life.

During this period, a warrior culture was becoming dominant and an aristocratic class began to control the imperial court. Literature flourished because the aristocratic clans needed an educated class to carry out the work of running the country.

3.1 POSSESSION AND EXORCISM

Given the spread of literacy during the Heian period, it is not surprising that what might well be the world's first novel should appear. And it is not surprising that this novel should have to do with court life and the romantic affairs of a prince named Genji. What is surprising is that the novel has both a modern ring to it and that it was written by a woman. Her nickname was Murasaki Shikibu, and she was born about 973 to a midlevel aristocratic family. Shikibu means "Bureau of Ceremonial," and Murasaki is the name of the fictional heroine of her eleventh-century novel titled *Tale of Genji*.

The excerpt that follows is an account of the possession of Aoi, Prince Genji's wife, by a "malign spirit" that turns out to be the Rokujo lady with whom Prince Genji has been having an affair. The situation is complicated by the fact that Aoi is about to give birth.

While this story is fiction, it reflects an aspect of real life. Belief in possession by evil spirits and rites of exorcism to cast them out were widespread in ancient

Japan and can be found in many places in the world today, including modern America. Shinto priests performed exorcisms, but it is interesting to note that this story portrays them as not particularly effective.

MURASAKI SHIKIBU

Tale of Genji

READING QUESTIONS

1. This story reflects certain kinds of beliefs about spirits and the dead. What are they?
2. How is it determined that the Rokujo lady's spirit was possessing Aoi?
3. What kinds of psychological and sociological explanations might be given for the possession of Aoi and the success, at least temporally, of the exorcism rite?
4. What do you think is the main point of this story?

At Sanjo, Genji's wife seemed to be in the grip of a malign spirit. It was no time for nocturnal wanderings. Genji paid only an occasional visit to his own Nijo mansion. His marriage had not been happy, but his wife was important to him and now she was carrying his child. He had prayers read in his Sanjo rooms. Several malign spirits were transferred to the medium and identified themselves, but there was one which quite refused to move. Though it did not cause great pain, it refused to leave her for so much as an instant. There was something very sinister about a spirit that eluded the powers of the most skilled exorcists. The Sanjo people went over the list of

Genji's ladies one by one. Among them all, it came to be whispered, only the Rokujo lady and the lady at Nijo seemed to have been singled out for special attentions, and no doubt they were jealous. The exorcists were asked about the possibility, but they gave no very informative answers. Of the spirits that did announce themselves, none seemed to feel any deep enmity toward the lady. Their behavior seemed random and purposeless. There was the spirit of her dead nurse, for instance, and there were spirits that had been with the family for generations and had taken advantage of her weakness.

The confusion and worry continued. The lady would sometimes weep in loud wailing sobs, and sometimes be tormented by nausea and shortness of breath.

The old emperor sent repeated inquiries and ordered religious services. That the lady should be worthy of these august attentions made the possibility of her death seem even more lamentable. Reports that they quite monopolized the attention of court reached the Rokujo mansion, to further embitter its lady. No one can have guessed that the trivial incident of the carriages had so angered a lady whose sense of rivalry had not until then been strong.

Not at all herself, she left her house to her daughter and moved to one where Buddhist rites would not be out of place.[1] Sorry to hear of the move, Genji bestirred himself to call on her. The neighborhood was a strange one and he was in careful disguise. He explained his negligence in terms likely to make it seem involuntary and to bring her forgiveness, and he told her of Aoi's illness and the worry it was causing him. . . .

The malign spirit was more insistent, and Aoi was in great distress. Unpleasant rumors reached the Rokujo lady, to the effect that it might be her spirit or that of her father, the late minister. Though she had felt sorry enough for herself, she had not wished ill to anyone; and might it be that the soul of one so lost in sad thoughts went wandering off by itself? She had, over the years, known the full range of sorrows, but never before had she felt so utterly miserable. There had been no release from the anger since the other lady had so insulted her, indeed behaved as if she did not exist. More than once she had the same dream: in the beautifully appointed apartments of a lady who seemed to be a rival she would push and shake the lady, and flail at her blindly and savagely. It was too terrible. Sometimes in a daze she would ask herself if her soul had indeed gone wandering off. The world was not given to speaking well of people whose transgressions had been far slighter. She would be notorious. It was common

enough for the spirits of the angry dead to linger on in this world. She had thought them hateful, and it was her own lot to set a hateful example while she still lived. She must think no more about the man who had been so cruel to her. But so to think was, after all, to think.

The high priestess, her daughter, was to have been presented at court the year before, but complications had required postponement. It was finally decided that in the Ninth Month she would go from court to her temporary shrine. The Rokujo house was thus busy preparing for two lustrations, but its lady, lost in thought, seemed strangely indifferent. A most serious state of affairs—the priestess's attendants ordered prayers. There were no really alarming symptoms. She was vaguely unwell, no more. The days passed. Genji sent repeated inquiries, but there was no relief from his worries about another invalid, a more important one.

It was still too early for Aoi to be delivered of her child. Her women were less than fully alert; and then, suddenly, she was seized with labor pains. More priests were put to more strenuous prayers. The malign spirit refused to move. The most eminent of exorcists found this stubbornness extraordinary, and could not think what to do. Then, after renewed efforts at exorcism, more intense than before, it commenced sobbing as if in pain.

"Stop for a moment, please. I want to speak to General Genji."

It was as they had thought. The women showed Genji to a place at Aoi's curtains. Thinking—for she did seem on the point of death—that Aoi had last words for Genji, her parents withdrew. The effect was grandly solemn as priests read from the Lotus Sutra in hushed voices. Genji drew the curtains back and looked down at his wife. She was heavy with child, and very beautiful. Even a man who was nothing to her would have been saddened to look at her. Long, heavy hair, bound at one side, was set off by white robes, and he thought her lovelier than when she was most carefully dressed and groomed.

He took her hand. "How awful. How awful for you." He could say no more.

Usually so haughty and forbidding, she now gazed up at him with languid eyes that were presently filled with tears. How could he fail to be moved? This violent weeping, he thought, would be for her parents, soon to be left behind, and perhaps, at this last leave-taking, for him too.

"You mustn't fret so. It can't be as bad as you think. And even if the worst comes, we will meet again. And your good mother and father: the bond between parents and children lasts through many lives. You must tell yourself that you will see them again."

"No, no. I was hurting so, I asked them to stop for a while. I had not dreamed that I would come to you like

---

this. It is true: a troubled soul will sometimes go wandering off." The voice was gentle and affectionate.

Bind the hem of my robe, to keep it within,
The grieving soul that has wandered through the skies.

It was not Aoi's voice, nor was the manner hers. Extraordinary—and then he knew that it was the voice of the Rokujo lady. He was aghast. He had dismissed the talk as vulgar and ignorant fabrication, and here before his eyes he had proof that such things did actually happen. He was horrified and repelled.

"You may say so. But I don't know who you are. Identify yourself."

It was indeed she. "Aghast"—is there no stronger word? He waved the women back.

Thinking that these calmer tones meant a respite from pain, her mother came with medicine; and even as she drank it down she gave birth to a baby boy. Everyone was delighted, save the spirits that had been transferred to mediums. Chagrined at their failure, they were raising a great stir, and all in all it was a noisy and untidy scene. There was still the afterbirth to worry about. Then, perhaps because of all the prayers, it too was delivered. The grand abbot of Hiei and all the other eminent clerics departed, looking rather pleased with themselves as they mopped their foreheads. Sure that the worst was past after all the anxious days, the women allowed themselves a rest.

The prayers went on as noisily as ever, but the house was now caught up in the happy business of ministering to a pretty baby. It hummed with excitement on each of the festive nights. Fine and unusual gifts came from the old emperor and from all the princes and high courtiers. Ceremonies honoring a boy baby are always interesting.

The Rokujo lady received the news with mixed feelings. She had heard that her rival was critically ill, and now the crisis had passed. She was not herself. The strangest thing was that her robes were permeated with the scent of the poppy seeds burned at exorcisms. She changed clothes repeatedly and even washed her hair, but the odor persisted. She was overcome with self-loathing. And what would others be thinking? It was a matter she could discuss with no one. She could only suffer in distraught silence.

Somewhat calmer, Genji was still horrified at the unsolicited remarks he had had from the possessive spirit. He really must get off a note to the Rokujo lady. Or should he have a talk with her? He would find it hard to be civil, and he did not wish to hurt her. In the end he made do with a note. . . .

The Sanjo mansion was almost deserted. Aoi was again seized with a strangling shortness of breath; and very soon after a messenger had been sent to court she

was dead. Genji and the others left court, scarcely aware of where their feet were taking them. Appointments and promotions no longer concerned them. Since the crisis had come at about midnight there was no possibility of summoning the grand abbot and his suffragans. Everyone had thought that the worst was over, and now of course everyone was stunned, dazed, wandering aimlessly from room to room, hardly knowing a door from a wall. Messengers crowded in with condolences, but the house was in such confusion that there was no one to receive them. The intensity of the grief was almost frightening. Since malign spirits had more than once attacked the lady, her father ordered the body left as it was for two or three days in hopes that she might revive. The signs of death were more and more pronounced, however, and, in great anguish, the family at length accepted the truth. Genji, who had private distress to add to the general grief, thought he knew as well as anyone ever would what unhappiness love can bring. Condolences even from the people most important to him brought no comfort. The old emperor, himself much grieved, sent a personal message; and so for the minister there was new honor, happiness to temper the sorrow. Yet there was no relief from tears.

Every reasonable suggestion was accepted toward reviving the lady, but, the ravages of death being ever more apparent, there was finally no recourse but to see her to Toribe Moor [for burial].

3.2 RITUAL PURIFICATION

We are tempted to think of pollution and purification of a person in moral terms. Pollution is morally bad while purification is morally good. This is too simplistic. Becoming polluted may involve breaking certain moral norms, but it may also involve doing something or coming in contact with something that has little to do with morality. For example, dust can be considered polluting, as can association with "unclean" social groups, women during menstruation, and the dead. Polluting oneself involves transgressing social and cultural taboos, but what lies at the heart of the action is the transgression of boundaries that are considered both natural and sacred. Superhuman powers have set limits relating to such things as what people can eat, who they can marry, and what they can say. To mix categories that sacred powers have separated and to overstep the boundaries they have set is to risk pollution of the self. Breaking divine regulations is dangerous not only to the person who does it but also to the whole community.

There are many boundaries and hence many opportunities for a person to become what is considered "polluted." Thus, a general purification covering all possible contact with polluting elements periodically needs to be performed. In Shintoism, a "Great Exorcism" or purification ritual is performed at midyear and year's end. Below is an example of a *norito*, a ritual prayer designed to purify all. This ritual was intended not only to purify the people but the animals and the land as well. People believed the kami worked through the forces of wind and water to remove "sins" or impurities.

TRANSLATED BY
DONALD L. PHILIPPI

Great Exorcism of the Last Day of the Sixth Month

READING QUESTIONS

1. Outline the structure of the Great Exorcism prayer. Does your outline reveal anything that you did not see when you first read it?
2. What are the social functions of the Great Exorcism?
3. How does this prayer remind people of the classical mythology expressed in the *Kojiki?*
4. Characterize the logic behind the way in which the pollutants ("sins") are disposed?

Hear me, all of you assembled princes of the blood, princes, court nobles, and all officials. Thus I speak.

The various sins perpetrated and committed
    By those who serve in the Emperor's court,
        The scarf-wearing women attendants,
        The sash-wearing men attendants,
        The quiver-bearing guard attendants,
        The sword-bearing guard attendants,
    As well as all those who serve in various offices—
These sins are to be exorcised, are to be purified
    In the great exorcism of the last day of the sixth month of this year—

From "Great Exorcism of the Last Day of the Sixth Month," in *Norito: A New Translation of the Ancient Japanese Ritual Prayers,* translated by Donald L. Philippi. Copyright © 1991 Princeton University Press. Reprinted by permission of Princeton University Press.

Hear me, all of you. Thus I speak.

By the command of the Sovereign Ancestral Gods and Goddesses,
    Who divinely remain in the High Heavenly Plain,
The eight myriad deities were convoked in a divine convocation,
    Consulted in a divine consultation,
    And spoke these words of entrusting:
        'Our Sovereign Grandchild is to rule
        'The Land of the Plentiful Reed Plains of the Fresh Ears of Grain
        'Tranquilly as a peaceful land.'
Having thus entrusted the land,
    They inquired with a divine inquiry
    Of the unruly deities in the land,
    And expelled them with a divine expulsion;
They silenced to the last leaf
    The rocks and the stumps of the trees,
    Which had been able to speak,
And caused him to descend from the heavens,
    Leaving the heavenly rock-seat,
    And pushing with an awesome pushing
        Through the myriad layers of heavenly clouds—
Thus they entrusted [the land to him].

The lands of the four quarters thus entrusted,
    Great Yamato, the Land of the Sun-Seen-on-High,
    Was pacified and made a peaceful land;
The palace posts were firmly planted in the bed-rock below,
    The cross-beams soaring high towards the High Heavenly Plain,
    And the noble palace of the Sovereign Grandchild constructed,
        Where, as a heavenly shelter, as a sun-shelter, he dwells hidden,
        And rules [the kingdom] tranquilly as a peaceful land.

The various sins perpetrated and committed
    By the heavenly ever-increasing people to come into existence
    In this land which he is to rule tranquilly as a peaceful land:
First, the heavenly sins:
    Breaking down the ridges,
    Covering up the ditches,
    Releasing the irrigation sluices,
    Double planting,
    Setting up stakes,
    Skinning alive, skinning backwards,
    Defecation—
Many sins [such as these] are distinguished and called the heavenly sins.

The earthly sins:
    Cutting living flesh, cutting dead flesh,
    White leprosy, skin excrescences,
    The sin of violating one's own mother,
    The sin of violating one's own child,
    The sin of violating a mother and her child,
    The sin of violating a child and her mother,
    The sin of transgression with animals,
    Woes from creeping insects,
    Woes from the deities of on high,
    Woes from the birds of on high,
    Killing animals, the sin of witchcraft—
    Many sins [such as these] shall appear.

When they thus appear,
By the heavenly shrine usage,
    Let the Great Nakatomi cut off the bottom and cut
      off the top
      Of heavenly narrow pieces of wood,
    And place them in abundance on a thousand
      tables;
    Let him cut off the bottom and cut off the top
      Of heavenly sedge reeds
    And cut them up into myriad strips;
    And let him pronounce the heavenly ritual, the
      solemn ritual words.
When he thus pronounces them,
    The heavenly deities will push open the heavenly
      rock door,
    And pushing with an awesome pushing
      Through the myriad layers of heavenly clouds,
    Will hear and receive [these words].
Then the earthly deities will climb up
    To the summits of the high mountains and to the
      summits of the low mountains,
    And pushing aside the mists of the high mountains
      and the mists of the low mountains,
    Will hear and receive [these words].

When they thus hear and receive,
Then, beginning with the court of the Sovereign
    Grandchild,
    In the lands of the four quarters under the heavens,
    Each and every sin will be gone.
As the gusty wind blows apart the myriad layers of
    heavenly clouds;
    As the morning mist, the evening mist is blown away
      by the morning wind, the evening wind;
    As the large ship anchored in the spacious port is
      untied at the prow and untied at the stern
        And pushed out into the great ocean;

As the luxuriant clump of trees on yonder [hill]
    Is cut away at the base with a tempered sickle, a
      sharp sickle—
As a result of the exorcism and the purification,
    There will be no sins left.
They will be taken into the great ocean
    By the goddess called Se-ori-tu-hime,
    Who dwells in the rapids of the rapid-running rivers
      Which fall surging perpendicular
      From the summits of the high mountains and the
      summits of the low mountains.
When she thus takes them,
    They will be swallowed with a gulp
      By the goddess called Haya-aki-tu-hime,
        Who dwells in the wild brine, the myriad
        currents of the brine,
          In the myriad meeting-place of the brine of
          the many briny currents.
When she thus swallows them with a gulp,
    The deity called Ibuki-do-nusi,
      Who dwells in the Ibuki-do,*
    Will blow them away with his breath to the land of
      Hades, the under-world.
When he thus blows them away,
    The deity called Haya-sasura-hime,
      Who dwells in the land of Hades, the
      under-world,
    Will wander off with them and lose them.
When she thus loses them,
    Beginning with the many officials serving in the
      Emperor's court,
    In the four quarters under the heavens,
    Beginning from today,
    Each and every sin will be gone.
Holding the horses
    Which stand listening,
      Pricking up their ears towards the High
      Heavenly Plain,
Hear me, all of you:
Know that [all the sins] have been exorcised and
  purified
    In the great exorcism performed in the waning of
      the evening sun
    On the last day of the sixth month of this year.
    Thus I speak.

Oh diviners of the four lands,
    Carry them out to the great river
    And cast them away. Thus I speak.

———————
* lit., Breath-blowing-entrance

4

Kamakura Period (1192–1333)

The Mongols attempted to invade Japan in 1274 and 1281, but due to typhoon winds were driven back. This seemingly miraculous deliverance led to the designation of the winds as **kamikaze** or winds sent by the kami to save the sacred islands of Japan. This reinforced the people's sense of living in a country in which divine providence had a special interest (a sense not unknown to other nations) and in World War II kamikaze became the name for suicide bombers who defended Japan by crashing their planes into enemy ships.

The Kamakura period was a turbulent time. In addition to the attempted invasion of the Mongols, the Hojo regent seized political power and the shogunate (rule by military governors) was established. Chinese Chan (meditation) masters emigrated to Japan establishing Zen Buddhism and a number of great Buddhist religious leaders emerged, including Dogen and Nichiren. People thought that they were living in the "end times." Some great cosmic catastrophe seemed just around the corner. Troubled times often spark eschatological dreams of escape. Buddhist movements such as Jodo (Pure Land) and Nichiren's relentless preaching on how corrupt and degenerate the world had become fueled these dreams.

4.1 PILGRIMAGE

Pilgrimages to sacred places are popular at any time but during times of stress and trouble they become even more popular. Among the countless Shinto shrines, the Grand Shrine of Ise is primary. Many Japanese view a pilgrimage to this site at least once in their lives as a sacred obligation. The emperor established a shrine at Ise around 300 when he sought a proper place for the worship for the Sun Goddess Amaterasu. Traditionally, a princess of the imperial family served as head priestess at the shrine. The goddess of harvest, Toyouke, was later moved to Ise to provide Amaterasu both food and company.

Today, Ise is a shrine complex consisting of an outer shrine devoted to Toyouke and an inner shrine devoted to Amaterasu. Every twenty years, the Ise Shrine is rebuilt so that it is kept fresh and new for the ancient kami who live there. This expensive and elaborate rebuilding according to exacting ancient standards ensures that traditional artisanship is passed on from one generation to another.

Fortunately, we have a diary (see below) from a Buddhist priest named Saka who made the pilgrimage to Ise in the fourteenth century. The fact that a Buddhist would undertake this journey to a sacred Shinto site attests to the close relationship between Shintoism and Buddhism during medieval times. However, the fact that there are rules, which Saka obeys, prohibiting Buddhist priests from getting too close to the shrine may indicate a growing sense of the differences between Buddhism and Shintoism.

TRANSLATED BY A. L. SADLER

Saka's Diary of a Pilgrim to Ise

READING QUESTIONS

1. Why do you think that the Imperial Palace would not let Buddhist monks go to certain parts of the shrine?
2. Why do you think a Buddhist monk whose access is limited would want to make a pilgrimage to a Shinto shrine in the first place?

From *The Ise Daijingu Sankeiki* or *Diary of a Pilgrim to Ise*, translated by A. L. Sadler. Reprinted by permission of the Estate of A. L. Sadler. Most footnotes omitted.

3. What is the difference between inner and outer purity, and why did this information cause Saka to shed tears of gratitude?
4. What is the significance of the Sacred Mirror?

When on the way to these Shrines one does not feel like an ordinary person any longer but as though reborn in another world. How solemn is the unearthly shadow of the huge groves of ancient pines and chamaecyparis (C. Obtusa, Setz), and there is a delicate pathos in the few rare flowers that have withstood the winter frosts so gaily. The cross-beams of the Torii or Shintō gate way is without any curve, symbolizing by its straightness the sincerity of the direct beam of the Divine promise. The shrine-fence is not painted red nor is the Shrine itself roofed with cedar shingles. The eaves, with their rough reed-thatch, recall memories of the ancient days when the roofs were not trimmed. So did they spare expense out of compassion for the hardships of the people. Within the Shrine there are many buildings where the festival rites are performed, constructed just like those in the Imperial Palace. Buddhist monks may go only as far as the Sacred Tree known as the Cryptomeria of the Five Hundred Branches (Ioe-no-sugi). They may not go to the Shrine. This, too, is a ceremonial rule of the Imperial Court.

The Divine Descendants received the Sovereignty and were proclaimed Emperors and the Imperial Ancestress was venerated and called the Great Deity. And the benevolent grace that gives to this land peace and security is that which radiates from the all-protecting Ancestral Shrine. And thinking over this I wrote:

When we consider
The forbear of our Sovereigns,
Deity of ancient Ise,
We see then how this place is
The Capital of the Deity.

But though the high cross-beams and roof-trees have stood here throughout the seasons for a thousand moons or more, the Shrine and torii or Shintō gate way have really not yet seen twenty autumns. As peace and order in the province has only just been restored, it is quite natural that the rebuilding is not begun yet. . . .

When I went to worship at the Shrine of the Moon-Deity Tsukiyomi the fallen leaves in the grove covered my traces and the winter powdered the foliage in the court. And the name of Tsukiyomi recalled so vividly the age of the deities that I was inspired to write:

How many long years
Has this ancient shrine-fence stood

Wet with countless dews,
And the Moon of the Gods' Age
Is this selfsame autumn moon.

I fear that my clumsy pen can hardly do justice to the road from Yamada to the Inner Shrine. Sometimes the spray over the hills seems to reflect their reversed silhouettes, sometimes the way is shrouded in cloud so that the countless peaks of the hills are hidden. As we approach the village of Uji the name is welcome to us with its suggestion of nearness to the Capital, and as it lies under the hills at the south-west of the Outer Shrine it is a place where you might imagine people would make cottages to live in retirement. As we went on deep in the shade of the chamaecyparis groves there was not even the smoke of any habitation to be seen, and we felt as though we had suddenly transcended the bounds of this painful world, while the hills with their cloud-capped mystery transported us to the world of Taoist fairyland.

When I entered the second Torii or Shintō Gate Way to worship it was dark under the pines at the foot of the hill and the branches were so thick-matted that one could hardly discern "the Pine of one hundred branches." The cryptomerias within the Shrine precincts were so dense that even the oblique projecting roof-beams could hardly be made out. When I come to reflect on my condition my mind is full of the Ten Evils[1] and I felt shame at so long forsaking the will of Buddha, yet as I wear one of the three monkish robes[2] I must feel some chagrin at my estrangement from the Way of the Deities.

And particularly is it the deeply-rooted custom of this Shrine that we should bring no Buddhist rosary or offering, or any special petition in our hearts and this is called "Inner Purity." Washing in sea water and keeping the body free from all defilement is called "Outer Purity." And when both these Purities are attained there is then no barrier between our mind and that of the Deity. And if we feel to become thus one with the Divine, what more do we need and what is there to pray for? When I heard that this was the true way of worshipping at the Shrine, I could not refrain from shedding tears of gratitude.

That which embodies the Deity in the Inner Shrine is the Sacred Mirror. It was cast in the heavens by the

---

[1] Ten Evils. The famous Ten Buddhist Categories or Commandments. Killing, Theft and Adultery (body), Lying, Boasting, Abuse, Ambiguity (mouth), and Covetousness, Malice and Scepticism (mind).
[2] One of the three monkish robes. As a physician Saka had to be a Buddhist monk and dressed as one, therefore he could only worship from afar from the Shrine.

eight million deities. And it is written that when Ama-terasu-ōmi-kami secluded herself in the Heavenly Rock Cave utter darkness took possession of the world. Then the deities assembled, and on the uprooted Sakaki of Mt. Kagu (Kagu-yama) they hung a mirror and jewels and the blue and white soft hempen cloths. And when they sang and danced the Kagura or divine dance and the Sun-Goddess opened the door of the cave a little to look out, the Deity Tajikarao-no-mikoto pushed it back and drew her forth so that her August Figure was reflected in the mirror.

And since the time of the first Sovereign, Jimmu Tennō, this mirror abode in the Palace but Sujin Tennō, the tenth Mikado, overcome by awe at its presence, had a separate shrine made for it where it was installed for worship, and this is called the Unmeiden. . . .

4.2 OF GODS AND RULERS

Buddhism and Shintoism had mixed so well in Japan that it was very difficult to tell where Buddhism ended and Shintoism began during the Kamakura period. The boundaries were fluid and, for most people, of little importance. In many cases, Buddhist priests served Shinto shrines and, as mentioned in the previous reading, made pilgrimages to Shinto holy sites. Buddhism came to dominate much of court life and hence much of the politics of Japan. The influence of Buddhism steadily increased during the Kamakura era with the rise of a number of Buddhists sects such as Pure Land Buddhism, Rinzai and Soto Zen, and Nichiren Buddhism. Collectively, these sects came to be called "Kamakura Buddhism" and were very successful in attracting converts because they preached an egalitarian message of salvation to all people rich or poor, male or female.

The growing influence of Kamakura Buddhism led to resentment in some circles. A scholar named Kitabatake Chikafusa (1293–1354), living near the end of the Kamakura period, began to articulate a view of Shinto that bound it closer to the imperial line, the land of Japan, and the politics of the country. He proclaimed Shinto to be the original and unique Japanese religion, thereby sowing the seeds of what would eventually develop into the view that Shinto and the kami not only made Japan unique, but also superior to other countries. In the following selection, Kitabatake Chikafusa articulates some of his views on Shinto and Japan.

KITABATAKE CHIKAFUSA

A Chronicle of Gods and Sovereigns

READING QUESTIONS

1. How would you feel about your country if you believed that it was a divine land especially created by the divine for you and your fellow citizens?
2. What is the purpose of the author's comparisons to China and India?
3. Why is the unbroken imperial succession so important?
4. How does Kitabatake interpret the **three imperial regalia?** Would you say his interpretation is religious or political or both? Why?
5. How does Kitabatake subordinate Buddhism and Confucianism to Shinto without totally rejecting them?

Great Japan is the divine land. The heavenly progenitor founded it, and the sun goddess bequeathed it to her descendants to rule eternally. Only in our country is this true; there are no similar examples in other countries. This is why our country is called the divine land.

During the age of the gods, Japan was known as Toyoashi-hara-no-Chiiho-no-Aki-no-Mizuho-no-kuni. This name was used from the time when heaven and earth were separated, and can be found in the directive that the heavenly progenitor, Kuni-no-Tokotachi-no-mikoto, presented to the male and female deities Izanagi and Izanami. The name also appears in the mandate that the sun goddess, Amaterasu Ō-mikami, gave to her heavenly grandson, Ninigi. It may therefore be regarded as the original designation for our country.

Another name for Japan is the Land of Eight Great Islands (Ō-Yashima), which derives from the fact that Izanagi and Izanami created the country in the form of eight islands.

Still another name for Japan is Yamato, taken from a province in the middle of the Land of Eight Great Islands. The eighth deity produced by Izanagi and

From *A Chronicle of Gods and Sovereigns, the Jinno Shotoki of Kitabatake Chikafusa*, translated by H. Paul Varley (New York: Columbia University Press, 1980), 49–50, 60–61, 76–78. Copyright © 1980 Columbia University Press. Reprinted with permission of the publisher.

Izanami was Ame-no-Misora-Toyoakizune-wake, who was designated Ō-Yamato-Toyoakizu Island. Today this island (Honshu) is divided into forty-eight provinces, the most central of which is Yamato. Because of its centrality, Yamato served for generations after Emperor Jimmu's eastward campaign as the imperial seat; and because Yamato held the imperial seat, its name was applied as well to the rest of Japan . . .

The origin of things in our country, whereby the world was produced by the descendants of the gods on high, bears some resemblance to the creation story of India. A significant difference is that, from the time of the heavenly founder, Kuni-no-Tokotachi-no-mikoto, there has been no disruption in dynastic succession (*keitai*) in Japan. Rather, our country has been uninterruptedly ruled by the sovereigns of a single dynastic line. In India the first sovereign, the people's lord, was selected by the people and was succeeded by his descendants. But in later generations many members of the lord's line perished and even a man of mean origins, if he possessed the military power, could become king— or rise to be ruler of all India.

China is also a country that tends strongly toward disorder. In early times, when life in China was simple and the right way prevailed, men of wisdom were selected to occupy the imperial office. But no single, immutable dynastic line was founded, and whenever the country lapsed into disorder, people mustered their forces and contended for hegemony. Men arose from among the common people to become emperors, and there were also cases of barbarians who emerged and seized control of the country. In still other cases, hereditary vassals surpassed their lords and ultimately succeeded to the emperorships held by the latter. Since the time of the first ruler, Fu Hsi, there have been thirty-six dynastic changes in China. The resulting disorder has been unspeakable.

In our country alone, the imperial succession has followed in an unbroken line from the time when heaven and earth were divided until the present age. Although, as is inevitable within a single family, the succession has at times been transmitted collaterally (*katawara yori*), the principle has prevailed that it will invariably return to the direct (*sei*) line. This is entirely the result of the immutable mandate of Amaterasu, and is the reason why Japan differs from all other countries.

The way of the gods (*shintō*) is not readily revealed. Yet if the divine basis of things is not understood, such ignorance will surely give rise to disorder. To rectify the ignorance that is the cause of disorder, I have been motivated to take up my brush. Since my chief aim is to discuss the principles of direct succession (*shōri*) to the throne from the age of the gods, I shall omit discussion of matters that are commonly known. I have decided to name what I write "The Chronicle of the Direct Descent of Gods and Sovereigns." . . .

Before bestowing the imperial regalia upon Ninigi, Amaterasu addressed him with these words: "Ashihara-no-Chiiho-no-Aki-no-Mizuho-no-kuni is a land that shall be ruled by my descendants. Go there and rule. Go, and may your line prosper eternally, like heaven and earth." Taking the sacred mirror in her hand, Amaterasu intoned the prayer: "Whenever you look upon this mirror, may it be as though you are looking upon me. Keep it with you as your sacred mirror, in your bed and under your roof."

Thus the Yata mirror, the Yasakani jewels, and the Ame-no-Murakumo sword came to comprise the imperial regalia. Amaterasu further enjoined Ninigi: "As the mirror is bright, illuminate the world; as the jewels spread broadly, rule with their wonderful sway; and, with the sword, subdue all those who do not submit to your rule." We can clearly see in these decrees that the divine spirit of our country lies in the legitimate passage of the emperorship to the descendants of a single family. Transmission of the regalia through the generations is as fixed as the sun, moon, and stars in heaven. The mirror is the body of the sun; the jewels possess the essence of the moon; and the sword has the substance of the stars. These are surely facts of profound significance.

The sacred mirror, as I have said, is the Yata mirror made by Ishikoridome-no-mikoto. (There is a secret transmission of knowledge concerning the meaning of the word *yata*.) An *uragaki* states:

> According to *Shuo-wen*, the *ta* unit of measure is equal to the hand span of a medium-sized woman or eight *sun*. This is the same as the *shaku* unit of the Chou period in China. But there are also other secret traditions about the facts concerning the Yata mirror of the imperial regalia.

The jewels are the Yasakani jewels made by Tamanoya-no-mikoto, who is also called Ame-no-Akarutama (there is a secret tradition about Yasakani too); and the sword is the Murakumo sword, found by Susanoo-no-mikoto and presented to Amaterasu. Amaterasu's mandate on the imperial regalia informs us of the proper way for governing the country.

The mirror possesses nothing of its own, but with an unselfish spirit illuminates all things. There is nothing, good or bad, that is not reflected in it, and its virtue is to reveal all forms with perfect fidelity. The mirror is the source of honesty (*shōjiki*). The virtue of the jewels is gentleness and yielding, and they are the source of compassion. The sword, which is the font of wisdom, has as its virtue strength and resolution. Unless a ruler possesses the virtues of all three of the regalia, he will find it difficult indeed to govern the country. Amaterasu's mandate is clear: its words are concise, but their import is far-reaching. Should we not feel the greatest gratitude that the spirit of the mandate is embodied in the imperial regalia?

Among the regalia, the mirror is of central importance, and is to be revered as the god-body (*shōtai*) of the Imperial Shrine at Ise. The mirror takes the form of brightness. If one's nature is bright, then one will also possess compassion and resolution. Since the mirror is a true reflection of Amaterasu herself, she must have invested it with her most profound feelings. There is nothing brighter in heaven than the sun and the moon: when written characters were devised, "the word 'bright' was represented by joining the characters for sun and moon." Because Amaterasu is the divine spirit of the great sun, she governs the world with a brilliant virtue. This is something not readily explainable by the tenets of *yin* and *yang*, but which demands faith in both the revealed and unrevealed realms.

Sovereigns and ministers alike have received the bright light of divine descent, or they are the descendants of deities who received Amaterasu's mandate. Who does not look with awe upon this fact? The highest purpose of all learning, both Buddhist and Confucian, is to make people aware of this and to prevent them from going against the way upon which it is based. Dissemination of Buddhist and Confucian learning has been the force in propagating this way. We may liken it to catching a fish in a net: although only one mesh is needed, it is difficult to catch a fish without the aid of an entire net made of meshes. Confucian texts have been propagated since the time of Emperor Ōjin and the teachings of Buddhism have flourished since the age of Prince Shōtoku. Both Ōjin and Shōtoku were avatars of divine *kami* spirits and seem to have intended, in accordance with the wishes of Amaterasu, to spread and make people fully aware of the way of our country . . .

5

Tokugawa (Edo) Period (1600–1868)

Between the Kamakura period and the Tokugawa (also known as the Edo period), the idea that the kami were the protectors of Japan and had a special interest in its welfare and in its people became widespread. In 1549, the Jesuit Francis Xavier introduced Roman Catholic Christianity into Japan in the midst of what is sometimes called the Warring States period (1460–1573), when Japan was plunged into bloody civil wars among various warlords.

Social and political stability was restored as the shoguns took control of the country and established a capital in Edo (modern Tokyo) in 1603. The emergence of four distinct classes helped preserve stability—samurai (warriors), farmers, artisans, and merchants. The emperors remained as figureheads, but the real political and military power was in the hands of the shoguns. In order to insure social stability and avoid contamination from foreign influences, the ports of Japan were closed in 1639 and the persecution of Japanese Christians, which had begun in 1587, intensified. After signing a trade agreement with the United States in 1854, the ports were reopened in 1858 to trade with Western countries.

During the Tokugawa period the seeds were sown for a number of popular religious movements, some of which later blossomed as Shinto sects and then, in the last century, as new religions. Confucian learning flourished and Buddhism permeated Japanese culture more deeply. Thus, it is not surprising that the new religions were often a blend of Shinto, Confucian, Buddhist, Taoist, and Christian elements. However, there were reactions against this intermingling of different religious ideas and practices, as we shall shortly see.

5.1 NATIONAL LEARNING AND THE TRUE WAY

During the Tokugawa or Edo period many scholars sought to "restore" Shinto to what they imagined to be its former glory. These scholars were part of the

National Learning movement. Motoori Norinaga (1730–1801) was a major figure in this movement. He used careful philological methods to comb the *Kojiki* and other ancient documents in order to discover the "true way" and thereby revive a "Pure Shinto" that, he argued, foreign influence along with native neglect had obscured. Motoori and others believed that the dust of centuries had polluted the ancient Shinto traditions and that nothing less than purification was in order; purification conducted by the scholars of the National Learning movement as we see in the following selection.

MOTOORI NORINAGA

The True Tradition of the Sun Goddess

READING QUESTIONS

1. According to the author, what is the original Way?
2. Why has this "clear and explicit" Way been narrowly interpreted, thereby "depriving it of its comprehensive and primal character"?
3. What is the "special dispensation" of the "Imperial Land" and what does that mean for the special status of Japan?
4. What is the significance of the "Imperial Line" for Motoori?
5. What is the objection that the author considers, and how does he respond? Does his response remind you of similar arguments in other religions? If so, what are they?

From Motoori Norinaga, "The True Traditions of the Sun Goddess," edited by William Theodore de Bary, in *Sources of Japanese Tradition*, vol. II (New York: Columbia University Press, 1958), 15–18. Copyright © 1958 Columbia University Press. Reprinted by permission. Footnote omitted.

The True Way is one and the same, in every country and throughout heaven and earth. This Way, however, has been correctly transmitted only in our Imperial Land. Its transmission in all foreign countries was lost long ago in early antiquity, and many and varied ways have been expounded, each country representing its own way as the Right Way. But the ways of foreign countries are no more the original Right Way than end-branches of a tree are the same as its root. They may have resemblances here and there to the Right Way, but because the original truth has been corrupted with the passage of time, they can scarcely be likened to the original Right Way. Let me state briefly what that one original Way is. One must understand, first of all, the universal principle of the world. The principle is that Heaven and earth, all the gods and all phenomena, were brought into existence by the creative spirits of two deities—Takami-musubi and Kami-musubi. The birth of all humankind in all ages and the existence of all things and all matter have been the result of that creative spirit. It was the original creativity of these two august deities which caused the deities Izanagi and Izanami to create the land, all kinds of phenomena, and numerous gods and goddesses at the beginning of the Divine Age. This spirit of creativity [*musubi*, lit., "union"] is a miraculously divine act the reason for which is beyond the comprehension of the human intellect.

But in the foreign countries where the Right Way has not been transmitted this act of divine creativity is not known. Men there have tried to explain the principle of Heaven and earth and all phenomena by such theories as the yin and yang, the hexagrams of the Book of Changes, and the Five Elements. But all of these are fallacious theories stemming from the assumptions of the human intellect and they in no wise represent the true principle.

Izanagi, in deep sorrow at the passing of his goddess, journeyed after her to the land of death. Upon his return to the upper world he bathed himself at Ahagiwara in Tachibana Bay in Tsukushi in order to purify himself of the pollution of the land of death, and while thus cleansing himself, he gave birth to the Heaven-Shining Goddess who by the explicit command of her father-God, came to rule the Heavenly Plain for all time to come. This Heaven-Shining Goddess is none other than the sun in heaven which today casts its gracious light over the world. Then, an Imperial Prince of the Heaven-Shining Goddess was sent down from heaven to the middle kingdom of Ashihara. In the Goddess' mandate to the Prince at that time it was stated that his dynasty should be coeval with Heaven and earth. It is this mandate which is the very origin and basis of the Way. Thus,

all the principles of the world and the way of humankind are represented in the different stages of the Divine Age. Those who seek to know the Right Way must therefore pay careful attention to the stages of the Divine Age and learn the truths of existence. These aspects of the various stages are embodied in the ancient traditions of the Divine Age. No one knows with whom these ancient traditions began, but they were handed down orally from the very earliest times and they refer to the accounts which have since been recorded in the *Kojiki* and the *Nihongi*. The accounts recorded in these two scriptures are clear and explicit and present no cause for doubt. Those who have interpreted these scriptures in a later age have contrived oracular formulae and have expounded theories which have no real basis. Some have become addicts of foreign doctrines and have no faith in the wonders of the Divine Age. Unable to understand that the truths of the world are contained in the evolution of the Divine Age, they fail to ascertain the true meaning of our ancient tradition. As they base their judgment on the strength of foreign beliefs, they always interpret at their own discretion and twist to their own liking anything they encounter which may not be in accord with their alien teachings. Thus, they say that the High Heavenly Plain refers to the Imperial Capital and not to Heaven, and that the Sun Goddess herself was not a goddess nor the sun shining in the heavens but an earthly person and the forebear of the nation. These are arbitrary interpretations purposely contrived to flatter foreign ideologies. In this way the ancient tradition is made to appear narrow and petty, by depriving it of its comprehensive and primal character. This is counter to the meaning of the scriptures.

Heaven and earth are one; there is no barrier between them. The High Heavenly Plain is the high heavenly plain which covers all the countries of the world, and the Sun Goddess is the goddess who reigns in that heaven. Thus, she is without a peer in the whole universe, casting her light to the very ends of heaven and earth and for all time. There is not a single country in the world which does not receive her beneficent illuminations, and no country can exist even for a day or an hour bereft of her grace. This goddess is the splendor of all splendors. However, foreign countries, having lost the ancient tradition of the Divine Age, do not know the meaning of revering this goddess. Only through the speculations of the human intelligence have they come to call the sun and the moon the spirit of yang and yin. In China and other countries the "Heavenly Emperor" is worshiped as the supreme divinity. In other countries there are other objects of reverence, each according to its own way, but their teachings are based, some on the logic of inference, and some on arbitrary personal opinions. At any rate, they are merely man-made designations and the "Heavenly Ruler" or the "Heavenly Way" have no real existence at all. That foreign countries revere such nonexistent beings and remain unaware of the grace of the Sun Goddess is a matter of profound regret. However, because of the special dispensation of our Imperial Land, the ancient tradition of the Divine Age has been correctly and clearly transmitted in our country, telling us of the genesis of the great goddess and the reason for her adoration. The "special dispensation of our Imperial Land" means that ours is the native land of the Heaven-Shining Goddess who casts her light over all countries in the four seas. Thus our country is the source and fountainhead of all other countries, and in all matters it excels all the others. It would be impossible to list all the products in which our country excels, but foremost among them is rice, which sustains the life of man, for whom there is no product more important. Our country's rice has no peer in foreign countries, from which fact it may be seen why our other products are also superior. Those who were born in this country have long been accustomed to our rice and take it for granted, unaware of its excellence. They can enjoy such excellent rice morning and night to their heart's content because they have been fortunate enough to be born in this country. This is a matter for which they should give thanks to our shining deities, but to my great dismay they seem to be unmindful of it.

Our country's Imperial Line, which casts its light over this world, represents the descendants of the Sky-Shining Goddess. And in accordance with that Goddess' mandate of reigning "forever and ever, coeval with Heaven and earth," the Imperial Line is destined to rule the nation for eons until the end of time and as long as the universe exists. That is the very basis of our Way. That our history has not deviated from the instructions of the divine mandate bears testimony to the infallibility of our ancient tradition. It can also be seen why foreign countries cannot match ours and what is meant by the special dispensation of our country. Foreign countries expound their own ways, each as if its way alone were true. But their dynastic lines, basic to their existence, do not continue; they change frequently and are quite corrupt. Thus one can surmise that in everything they say there are falsehoods and that there is no basis in fact for them.

Objection: You are obstinate in insisting that the Sun Goddess is the sun in heaven. If this is so, perpetual darkness must have reigned everywhere before her birth. The sun must have been in heaven since the beginning of the universe [before the birth of the Goddess].

Motoori: First of all, I cannot understand why you say that I am obstinate. That the Sun Goddess is the sun in heaven is clear from the records of the *Kojiki* and the *Nihongi*. If it is so beyond any doubt, is not the person who raises an objection the one who is obstinate? This Sun Goddess casts her light to the very extremities of the universe, but in the beginning it was in our Imperial Land that she made her appearance, and as the sovereign of the Imperial Line, that is, of the Imperial Land, she has reigned supreme over the Four Seas until now. When this Goddess hid herself in a cave in heaven, closing its doors, darkness fell over the countries of the world. You ask why darkness did not reign everywhere before her birth, a question a child might well ask. It seems childish indeed when a question which might spring from the doubts of a child is asked with such insistence by you. But this very point proves that the ancient happenings of the Divine Age are facts and not fabrications. Some say that the records are the fabrication of later sovereigns, but who would fabricate such shallow sounding, incredible things? This is a point you should reflect upon seriously.

The acts of the gods cannot be measured by ordinary human reasoning. Man's intellect, however wise, has its limits. It is small, and what is beyond its confines it cannot know. The acts of the gods are straightforward. That they appear to be shallow and untrue is due to the limitation of what man can know. To the human mind these acts appear to be remote, inaccessible, and difficult of comprehension and belief. Chinese teachings, on the other hand, were established within the reach of human intelligence; thus, to the mind of the listener, they are familiar and intimate and easy of comprehension and belief. The Chinese, because they believe that the wisdom of the Sage [Confucius] was capable of comprehending all the truths of the universe and of its phenomena, pretend to the wisdom of the Sage and insist, despite their small and limited minds, that they know what their minds are really incapable of knowing. But at the same time they refuse to believe in the inscrutability of the truth, for this, they conclude, is irrational. This sounds clever, but on the contrary, it betrays the pettiness of their intelligence. If my objector would rid himself of such a habit and reflect seriously, such a doubt as he has just expressed would disappear of itself.

It will be recalled that when Izanagi made his way to the nether region, he carried a light because of the darkness there, but while he lived in the actual world, he did not. The nether world is dark because it has to be dark; the actual world is clear because it has to be clear. Thus, there was light in the actual world before the birth of the Sun Goddess, although the reason why it is so cannot be fathomed. In the commentaries on the *Nihongi* there are references to luminous human beings of the days of creation who cast light about them, but these references were derived from the Buddhist scriptures. There is also mention of a deity of firefly light, but this was an evil deity, and his case cannot be taken as a typical one. There are otherwise no traditions about deities of light, and thus we have no way of knowing what light there was for illumination. But presumably there was light for reasons beyond the reach of human intelligence. Why then did darkness prevail when the Sun Goddess hid herself behind the door of the rocky cave? It was because it had been determined that with the birth of the Sun Goddess the whole space of the universe should come within her illumination, and that henceforth there would be no light without her illumination. This is the same sort of inscrutable truth as the case of the descent of the Imperial Grandchild from Heaven after which communication between Heaven and earth was completely severed. There are many other strange and inscrutable happenings in the Divine Age, which should be accepted in the same way. The people of antiquity never attempted to reason out the acts of the gods with their own intelligence, but the people of a later age, influenced by the Chinese, have become addicts of rationalism. Such people appear wise, but in reality are quite foolish in their suspicion and skepticism about the strange happenings of the Divine Age which are quite different from the happenings of the human age. The fact is that even the things of the human age are, in reality, strange and wondrous, but because we are accustomed to their present form and have always lived in their midst, we cease to be aware of their wondrous quality. Consider, for example, how this universe goes on. Is the earth suspended in the sky or attached to something else? In either instance it is a wondrous thing. Suppose it is attached to something else, what is there under it to support it? This is something which cannot be understood.

5.2 THE BEGINNINGS OF A NEW RELIGION

A peasant woman, Nakayama Miki (1798–1887) was said to have become possessed by the Divine Reason Kami in 1839. Miki, as she came to be called, married and lived an ordinary peasant woman's life. When her son became ill, a shaman was called to perform an exorcism of the spirit causing the illness. This shaman worked with a female medium that experienced a temporary possession of a kami used in the

exorcism process. Because his usual medium was not available, Miki substituted and became permanently possessed by the Divine Reason Kami. This possession became the source of revelations and the founding event of a religious movement known as Tenrikyo (Way of Divine Reason).

Miki's fame spread rapidly after stories of her ability to give women an easy childbirth circulated. Her followers gave her the status of a "living-kami" and all that she did or said became sacred. Her message centered on the idea that God the Parent wanted people to live a joyous and happy life. However, selfish greed polluted people's minds and spirits. According to Miki, once people came to realize that their bodies were on "loan" from God the Parent, they would become capable of overcoming the pollution of selfishness. In order to help people overcome selfishness, Miki developed rituals of ecstatic dances that were said to help people rediscover their original joyous nature.

Although Miki had been raised as a devotee of Amida Buddha, her movement was recognized as one of the thirteen official sects of Shinto in 1908. It evolved over time into a unique combination of shamanistic, Buddhist, Shinto, and other elements. Today, many scholars regard Tenrikyo as a new religion in its own right. The following excerpts come from *The Doctrine of Tenrikyo*, an official statement of Tenrikyo teachings.

TRANSLATED BY JOSEPH M. KITAGAWA

The Doctrine of Tenrikyo

READING QUESTIONS

1. How does the kami who possesses Miki introduce himself?
2. What is meant by salvation and how is it attained?

From *The Great Asian Religions: An Anthology*, edited by Wing Tsit Chan, Joseph Kitigawa, et al. Copyright © 1969 by Prentice Hall Inc. Reprinted by permission of Pearson Education, Inc., Upper Saddle River, NJ.

3. What do you find significant about the cosmogony and why do you find it significant? What do you find puzzling and why? Can you identify any parallels in other myths that you know?
4. What are the eight kinds of mental dust?
5. What must humans realize, and what is the result of that realization?
6. What is a church?
7. What is the ultimate purpose of human existence, and how is it achieved?
8. Tenrikyo has become a very successful new religion with well over three million devotees. Why do you think it has become so successful?

1. THE REVELATION OF THE KAMI[1]

I, the foremost and true kami, have descended at this time from heaven to this house [of the Nakayama family] in order to save everyone of the world, and intend to dwell in the person of Miki as my living shrine. (*Tenri-kyō kyōten* [Doctrinal manual of Tenri-kyō], p. 3)

This world being based on reason, I am going to express my will through poetry. Since what I have spoken in the past might be forgotten, I have decided to reveal [my will] in the *Tip of the Writing Brush*.[2] (*Ibid.*, pp. 6–7)

Using the analogy of the road, I might say that beyond the mountain paths and thorny lanes along the cliff there is a narrow way. (*Ibid.*, p. 8)

In order to receive my assistance, you should not approach me with magical incantations and prayers, although it is permissible for you to inquire about my will. (*Ibid.*, p. 10)

My wish is like the concern of parents who try to help their children everyday. (*Ibid.*, p. 12)

2. SALVATION

I am going to perform something which is just as marvelous as the creation of the world by me. What I am going to initiate is a brand new type of a religious service. Should you wish to engage in a religious service, choose the service at the "sweet dew stand" [the central altar of Tenri-kyō]. I have placed the "sweet dew stand" [at the *jiba*, literally a "spot on earth," in Tenri City, Nara Prefecture] to indicate that I created human beings there. (*Ibid.*, pp. 16–17)

As for me, I can hardly wait for the next performance of "joyous service" [conducted around the "sweet dew stand"] which is nothing other than the service of sacred dance. (*Ibid.*, p. 18)

Performing this service is the way for mankind to be saved, whereby even the mute will begin to speak. Indeed, by diligently offering this service each day, you will avoid every kind of trouble. In fact, even the most serious sickness will be cured by performing the service diligently. (*Ibid.*, pp. 19–20)

Salvation, which to be sure depends on the sincerity of your heart, will not only enable you to prevent sickness but also death and decay. Indeed, if everyone united in mind should perform this service, all the problems of the world will be solved. Even the gravest sickness will be eliminated by the rhythmic breathing and hand gestures [of the sacred dance]. (*Ibid.*, pp. 20–22)

3. COSMOGONY

In the beginning of the world there was only an ocean of muddy waters. The divine parents, known then as the Moon-Sun, bored with the state of chaos, decided to create man in order to enjoy himself by looking at man's joyous life. He found in the muddy water a merman and snake mixed with a bunch of loaches, and brought them home by promising them that they would be venerated as kami. He then brought a dolphin and a sea-tiger in order to make them as the materials for the male and female elements, and inserted them into the merman and the snake, respectively, which he intended to use as the prototypes of man and woman. The seed of the man's prototype was given the sacred name of Kami-who-invites (Izanagi), while the seed-plot or potentiality of the prototype of woman was given the name of Kami-who-is-invited (Izanami). Besides, the principles of the functions of human bodies were given such names as Moon Kami and Kami of the Nation's Spirit. Next he called the eel, flat-fish, black snake, and globe-fish, and ate them in order to test their mental flavor, according to which these creatures were used for appropriate instruments of creation, such as the eel for ingressing and egressing, and the flat-fish for breathing and speaking.

The divine parent then ate all the loaches and decided to use them as the material for human beings. Now, the moon element of the divine parent entered the body of Izanagi, while the sun element entered the body of Izanami, both teaching them the art of human procreation. Meanwhile, 999,999 seeds were inserted into the womb of Izanami during the period of three

[1]His official name is Tenri-ō no Mikoto (Kami of Divine Reason), but is affectionately referred to as Oyasama (beloved parent), which is also used as the designation of the foundress.
[2]*Ofudesaki* in Japanese, one of the sacred writings of Tenri-kyō.

days and three nights, Izanami remained where she was for three years and three months, and it took seventy-five days for her to give birth to all these children.

The first group of offspring were all half an inch long at their birth, but grew half an inch at a time. After ninety-nine years they became about three inches long, and then all of them, as well as their father Izanagi, died. Then, Izanami, following the art of procreation which had been given her before, conceived the same number of seeds and delivered them after ten months. The offspring were again born half an inch long but grew to the height of three inches and a half after ninety-nine years, and then died. In her third attempt, the offspring were born half an inch long but grew to the height of four inches. Looking at them, Izanami smiled and said that they would eventually grow into human beings of five feet. She then died, and her offspring without exception followed her footsteps.

Subsequently, human beings went through 8,008 stages of rebirth, including those of the worm, birds, and animals, and eventually died out, leaving only one female monkey behind. From her womb, five men and five women were born. They were half an inch long at the time of birth but grew first to the height of eight inches and later to one foot and eight inches. About that time, by the operation of the divine parent, the muddy ocean began to be solidified, whereby ocean and mountains, heaven and earth, and sun and moon became differentiated. Meanwhile, many pairs of twins, each with male and female children, were born, and grew to the height of three feet. By that time, it became normal for one child at a time to be born from a mother's womb, and they also learned the art of speaking. When human beings reached the average height of five feet, they began to live on the ground.

[In retrospect, according to the scheme of the divine parent,] mankind lived the first period consisting of 990,000 years in water, and acquired intelligence during the second period consisting of 6,000 years. Finally, during the third period consisting of 3,999 years they learned the art of writing and reading letters. (*Ibid.*, pp. 25–29)

4. SOME CHARACTERISTIC CONCEPTS

"*Divine guidance.*" Although [one and the same] divine parent is shared by all mankind, human beings, not knowing this truth, fail to understand that all others are equally brothers and sisters who are the children of the divine parent. Thus, motivated by the false notion that each one lives only for his own sake, they tend to live with self-centred thinking and selfish actions, which harm and cloud others' minds and disrupt the harmony of the world. Moreover, they are unaware that [such a way of living] harms and clouds their own minds. The divine parent, concerned with his children who go astray along the dangerous paths, pities them, and tries to teach them as to who is their true parent as well as the way of joyous life which he wishes them to lead. In order to correct the misguided notions of human beings, [the divine parent] shows concrete signs in their lives. Thus, every kind of sickness, misfortune, and complication [of human relations] is the expression of paternal concern [of the divine parent] whose compassionate divine guidance leads men to the true joyous life. (*Ibid.*, pp. 57–59)

"*Lending and borrowing things.*" Inasmuch as we borrowed our life from the divine parent, it is essential that we use it to follow his will. (*Ibid.*, p. 65) But, human beings, not realizing this principle, tend to think that they can do everything according to their selfish desire based on their limited human minds. Preoccupied by their own suffering, happiness, and profit, human beings often think contrary to the will of [the divine parent] who wishes the harmony and happiness of all mankind. The divine parent warns men against such selfish concern by using the analogy of dust [which can easily accumulate and clouds our minds]. (*Ibid.*, p. 67) He cautions us to reflect on the eight kinds of mental dust—vindictiveness, possessiveness, hatred, self-centeredness, enmity, anger, greed, and arrogance. (*Ibid.*, p. 68) The important thing is for all of us to realize that we have borrowed our life and that it is [the divine parent who had lent it to us], and do not neglect the daily dusting of our minds. (*Ibid.*, p. 62)

"*Daily offering of labor.*" When one realizes his indebtedness to his divine parent concerning whatever happens in daily life, his grateful joy is automatically expressed in his attitudes and actions, [more concretely] in daily offering of labor. (*Ibid.*, p. 76) It does not refer to any [particular] activity but to daily, continuous, and joyful activities. Such a joy cannot be kept to one's own self only but is bound to influence others, so that all like-minded people will join together and share their joyfulness. (*Ibid.*, p. 78)

"*Timber.*" One's joy of having received salvation leads him to engage in activities to help others. In so doing, he becomes the "timber" [i.e., instrument] of the divine parent's enterprise to bring joyful life [to mankind]. (*Ibid.*, p. 84) When the effort of the "timber" bears fruit, whereby the seekers of the way gradually gather together, [such a group thus formed] will be given the title of a church. The life of a church should deepen the joyous happiness of the people, by their mutual assistance, wherever they may be, and become a model for the joyous life which would foster the mental growth [of all human beings]. (*Ibid.*, pp. 90–91)

"*Joyous life.*" When one spends each day diligently helping others, his heart will be filled with bright joyfulness because he is warmly embraced by the divine parent and rests in the sense of peacefulness derived from the assurance that he is saved by the act of helping others. This is the state of joyous life. The divine parent, be it remembered, created human beings in order to enjoy happiness with them by watching their joyous life. The fulfillment of his divine wish is the meaning of life and the ultimate purpose of human existence. (*Ibid.*, p. 92)

6

Meiji Restoration (1868–1945)

The Meiji Restoration refers to the restoration of the Emperor as the head of the emerging modern nation of Japan and the end of rule by the shoguns. The period marked wide-ranging changes in Japan. During that time, Japan began to move from a rural society to an urban society. An industrial economy started to replace an economy largely based on agriculture. Western ideas and practices permeated the society. In 1873, the Ban on Christianity was lifted, and in 1889 the Meiji Constitution was promulgated.

The Meiji Constitution officially proclaimed the separation of church and state and at the same time declared Shinto the national "faith" of Japan, thereby separating it from Buddhism and other religions. How can these two events go together? The solution was to distinguish between **State Shinto,** now proclaimed not to be a religion but to embody the traditional cultural values of the Japanese people, and **Sect Shinto,** which was considered religion. Thirteen official sects were recognized and designated religions. State economic support was given to State Shinto because it was officially not a religion, while Sect Shinto and other religious groups, such as the Buddhists and the Christians, had to survive without public funding. Ironically and unexpectedly the different religious groups flourished without state support in the free religious market created by distinguishing State from Sect Shinto.

Other distinctions within Shinto now became possible. Along with Sect Shinto and State Shinto, scholars often distinguish among **Folk** or **Popular Shinto, Domestic** or **Home Shinto, Imperial Household Shinto,** and **Shrine Shinto.** Folk Shinto usually refers to the kind of Shinto largely practiced in rural areas among the general populace. Domestic Shinto refers to the practices associated with home altars dedicated to the ancestors of the family or clan. Imperial Household Shinto designates the rites conducted by Shinto priests at the

three shrines within the palace grounds that center on the imperial kami ancestors. Shrine Shinto names the ritual practices conducted at the thousands of local shrines dedicated to various kami throughout Japan. Priests conduct services at these shrines and celebrate seasonal festivals. These services typically consist of purification rites, offerings to the kami, and prayers. They usually conclude with a symbolic feast called *naorai*, which means "to eat together with the kami." I have described key elements of Shinto worship as follows:

> The minimum requirement for worshiping the kami is periodic presentation of offerings. Many believe that the kami and particularly the ancestral spirits will be unhappy and bring misfortune if a devotee fails to observe this duty. As a rule the formal prayers recited by the priest open with words of praise for the kami and include petitions for favors, thanksgiving, a recitation of gifts offered, and the status and name of the priest. They usually close with words of awe and respect.*

6.1 EDUCATION AS PROPAGANDA

In order to make State Shinto work, the youth of Japan needed to be educated in its cardinal principles. Chief among these is loyalty to the emperor and hence to the state. Just as American pupils have been required to pledge allegiance to the flag and to the United States of America as one nation under God, so Japanese students were required to pledge allegiance to the emperor as the manifest kami, the visible symbol of Japanese traditional values.

---

*Gary E. Kessler, *Studying Religion: An Introduction Through Cases* (Boston: McGraw-Hill, 2003), 332.

The following reading is an official order or decree from the Meiji Restoration. It is called a rescript, and it concerns education. This official decree did not create the idea that one should be loyal to the emperor any more than the United States's pledge of allegiance created the idea that one ought to be loyal to the United States. Rather, it reinforced a tradition that was already well established.

TRANSLATED BY DAIROKU KIKUCHI

The Source of True Education

READING QUESTIONS

1. What is the source of education?
2. What virtues does this rescript teach, and how might these serve the interests of the state?
3. Are these virtues significantly different from the virtues you were taught in school?
4. How is the authority of the Shinto tradition used to reinforce the ideas expressed in this rescript?

Know ye, Our subjects:

Our Imperial Ancestors have founded Our Empire on a basis broad and everlasting, and have deeply and firmly implanted virtue; Our subjects ever united in loyalty and filial piety have from generation to generation illustrated the beauty thereof. This is the glory of the fundamental character of Our Empire, and herein also lies the source of Our education. Ye, Our subjects, be filial to your parents, affectionate to your brothers and sisters; as husbands and wives be harmonious, as friends true; bear yourselves in modesty and moderation; extend your benevolence to all; pursue learning and cultivate arts, and thereby develop intellectual faculties and perfect moral powers;

From Dairoku Kikuchi, *Japanese Education* (London: John Murray Publishers, 1909), 2–3.

furthermore, advance public good and promote common interests; always respect the Constitution and observe the laws; should emergency arise, offer yourselves courageously to the State; and thus guard and maintain the prosperity of Our Imperial Throne coeval with heaven and earth. So shall ye not only be Our good and faithful subjects, but render illustrious the best traditions of your forefathers.

The Way here set forth is indeed the teaching bequeathed by Our Imperial Ancestors, to be observed alike by Their Descendants and the subjects, infallible for all ages and true in all places. It is Our wish to lay it to heart in all reverence, in common with you, Our subjects, that we may all attain the same virtue.

The 30th day of the 10th month of the 23rd year of Meiji.
(The 30th of October, 1890).

(Imperial Sign Manual. Imperial Seal).

6.2 RELIGION AS IDEOLOGY

Between the *Rescript on Education* of 1890 and the 1937 publication of the *Kokutai no Hongi* or *Cardinal Principles of the National Entity of Japan*, Japan had fought and won two wars, the Sino-Japanese War of 1894–1895 and the Russo-Japanese War of 1904–1905. The rescript was an attempt to unify the people into a newly formed nation-state, but the government needed to gain support for the ever-expanding military goals of the Japanese nation. An appeal to the Shinto religion served its purposes well.

Politicians frequently appeal to religion in order to get people to make the sacrifices war requires. In these situations, religion becomes an ideology that serves nonreligious ends. The arguments government officials use are not unique to Japan, nor particularly new. They generally include at least two elements. First, the problems of the country are blamed on foreign influences and second, an appeal is made to recover a lost or corrupted moral and religious tradition. Unquestioning loyalty to the state even unto death becomes a key virtue and patriotism is elevated to a religious virtue. A selection from *Cardinal Principles* follows.

TRANSLATED BY
JOHN OWEN GAUNTLETT

Cardinal Principles of the National Entity of Japan

READING QUESTIONS

1. What are the sources of the social evils of Japan?
2. What do you think the author means by the "deadlock of individualism," and what contribution can Japan make to overcoming that deadlock?
3. What is the "Way of loyalty"?
4. How is ancient Shinto mythology used to support Japanese nationalism?
5. What is *Bushido?*
6. What does the author mean by "sublimating and assimilating Occidental ideologies"?

The various ideological and social evils of present-day Japan are the fruits of ignoring the fundamentals and of running into the trivial, of lack in sound judgment, and of failure to digest things thoroughly; and this is due to the fact that since the days of Meiji so many aspects of European and American culture, systems, and learning, have been imported, and that, too rapidly. As a matter of fact, foreign ideologies imported into our country are in the main the ideologies of enlightenment that have come down since the eighteenth century, or their extensions. The views of the world and of life that form the basis of these ideologies are a rationalism and a positivism, lacking in historical views, which on the one hand lay the highest value on, and assert the liberty and equality of, individuals, and on the other hand lay value on a world by nature abstract, transcending nations and races. Consequently, importance is laid upon human beings and their gatherings, who have become isolated from historical entireties, abstract and independent of each other. It is political, social, moral, and pedagogical

From *Kokutai no Hongi: Cardinal Principles of the National Entity of Japan*, translated by John Owen Gauntlett, and edited with an introduction by Robert King Hall (Cambridge, MA: Harvard University Press, 1949), 52, 54–55, 81–82, 87–88, 144–145, 175, 178. Copyright © 1949 by the President and Fellows of Harvard College. Copyright renewed 1977 by Robert King Hall. Reprinted by permission of the publisher.

theories based on such views of the world and of life, that have on the one hand made contributions to the various reforms seen in our country, and on the other have had deep and wide influence on our nation's primary ideology and culture. . . .

Paradoxical and extreme conceptions, such as socialism, anarchism, and communism, are all based in the final analyses on individualism which is the root of modern Occidental ideologies, and are no more than varied forms of their expressions. In the Occident, too, where individualism forms the basis of their ideas, they have, when it comes to communism, been unable to adopt it; so that now they are about to do away with their traditional individualism, which has led to the rise of totalitarianism and nationalism and incidentally to the upspringing of Fascism and Nazism. That is, it can be said that both in the Occident and in our country the deadlock of individualism has led alike to a season of ideological and social confusion and crisis. We shall leave aside for a while the question of finding a way out of the present deadlock, for, as far as it concerns our country, we must return to the standpoint peculiar to our country, clarify our immortal national entity, sweep aside everything in the way of adulation, bring into being our original condition, and at the same time rid ourselves of bigotry, and strive all the more to take in and sublimate Occidental culture; for we should give to basic things their proper place, giving due weight to minor things, and should build up a sagacious and worthy Japan. This means that the present conflict seen in our people's ideas, the unrest in their modes of life, the confused state of civilization, can be put right only by a thorough investigation by us of the intrinsic nature of Occidental ideologies and by grasping the true meaning of our national entity. Then, too, this should be done not only for the sake of our nation but for the sake of the entire human race which is struggling to find a way out of the deadlock with which individualism is faced. Herein lies our grave cosmopolitan mission. It is for this reason that we have compiled the *Cardinal Principles of the National Entity of Japan*, to trace clearly the genesis of the nation's foundation, to define its great spirit, to set forth clearly at the same time the features the national entity has manifested in history, and to provide the present generation with an elucidation of the matter, and thus to awaken the people's consciousness and their efforts. . . .

Our country is established with the Emperor, who is a descendant of Amaterasu Ohmikami, as her center, and our ancestors as well as we ourselves constantly behold in the Emperor the fountainhead of her life and activities. For this reason, to serve the Emperor and to receive the Emperor's great august Will as one's own is the rationale of making our historical "life" live in the present; and on this is based the morality of the people.

Loyalty means to reverence the Emperor as [our] pivot and to follow him implicitly. By implicit obedience is meant casting ourselves aside and serving the Emperor intently. To walk this Way of loyalty is the sole Way in which we subjects may "live," and the fountainhead of all energy. Hence, offering our lives for the sake of the Emperor does not mean so-called self-sacrifice, but the casting aside of our little selves to live under his august grace and the enhancing of the genuine life of the people of a State. The relationship between the Emperor and the subjects is not an artificial relationship [which means] bowing down to authority, nor a relationship such as [exists] between master and servant as is seen in feudal morals. . . . The ideology which interprets the relationship between the Emperor and his subjects as being a reciprocal relationship such as merely [involves] obedience to authority or rights and duties, rests on individualistic ideologies, and is a rationalistic way of thinking that looks on everything as being in equal personal relationships. An individual is an existence belonging to a State and her history which form the basis of his origin, and is fundamentally one body with it. . . .

In our country, the two Augustnesses, Izanagi no Mikoto and Izanami no Mikoto, are ancestral deities of nature and the deities, and the Emperor is the divine offspring of the Imperial Ancestor who was born of the two Augustnesses. The Imperial Ancestor and the Emperor are in the relationship of parent and child, and the relationship between the Emperor and his subjects is, in its righteousness, that of sovereign and subject and, in its sympathies, that of father and child. This relationship is an "essential" relationship that is far more fundamental than the rational, obligatory relationships, and herein are the grounds that give birth to the Way of loyalty. From the point of individualistic personal relationships, the relationship between sovereign and subject in our country may [perhaps] be looked upon as that between non-personalities. However, this is nothing but an error arising from treating the individual as supreme, from the notion that has individual thoughts for its nucleus, and from abstract consciousness. Our relationship between sovereign and subject is by no means a shallow, lateral relationship such as [means] the correlation between ruler and citizen, but is a relationship springing from a basis transcending this correlation, and is that of self-effacement and a return

to [the] "one," in which this basis is not lost. This is a thing that can never be understood from an individualistic way of thinking. In our country, this great Way has seen a natural development since the founding of the nation, and the most basic thing that has manifested itself as regards the subjects is in short this Way of loyalty. Herein exists the profound meaning and lofty value of loyalty. Of late years, through the influence of the Occidental individualistic ideology, a way of thinking which has for its basis the individual has become lively. Consequently, this and the true aim of our Way of loyalty which is "essentially" different from it are not necessarily [mutually] consistent. That is, those in our country who at the present time expound loyalty and patriotism are apt to lose [sight of] its true significance, being influenced by Occidental individualism and rationalism. We must sweep aside the corruption of the spirit and the clouding of knowledge that arises from setting up one's "self" and from being taken up with one's "self" and return to a pure and clear state of mind that belongs intrinsically to us as subjects, and thereby fathom the great principle of loyalty. . . .

In our country filial piety is a Way of the highest importance. Filial piety originates with one's family as its basis, and in its larger sense has the nation for its foundation. Filial piety directly has for its object one's parents, but in its relationship toward the Emperor finds a place within loyalty.

The basis of the nation's livelihood is, as in the Occident, neither the individual nor husband and wife. It is the home. . . .

The life of a family in our country is not confined to the present life of a household of parents and children, but beginning with the distant ancestors, is carried on eternally by the descendants. The present life of a family is a link between the past and the future, and while it carries over and develops the objectives of the ancestors, it hands them over to its descendants. Herein also lies the reason why since of old a family name has been esteemed in our country. A family name is an honor to a household built up by one's ancestors, so that to stain this may be looked upon not only as a personal disgrace but as a disgrace to a family that has come down in one line linking the past, present, and future. Accordingly, the announcing of one's real name by a knight who has gone out to the battlefield was in the nature of an oath to fight bravely by speaking of one's ancestors and their achievements, so as not to cast a slur on the name of an esteemed family. . . .

Bushido may be cited as showing an outstanding characteristic of our national morality. In the world of warriors one sees inherited the totalitarian structure and spirit of the ancient clans peculiar to our nation.

Hence, though the teachings of Confucianism and Buddhism have been followed, these have been transcended. That is to say, though a sense of indebtedness binds master and servant, this has developed into a spirit of self-effacement and of meeting death with a perfect calmness. In this, it was not that death was made light of so much as that man tempered himself to death and in a true sense regarded it with esteem. In effect, man tried to fulfill true life by way of death. This means that rather than lose the whole by being taken up with and setting up oneself, one puts self to death in order to give full play to the whole by fulfilling the whole. Life and death are basically one, and the monistic truth is found where life and death are transcended. Through this is life, and through this is death. However, to treat life and death as two opposites and to hate death and to seek life is to be taken up with one's own interests, and is a thing of which warriors are ashamed. To fulfill the Way of loyalty, counting life and death as one, is *Bushido*. . . .

We have inquired into the fundamental principles of our national entity and the ways in which it has been manifested in our national history. What kind of resolve and attitude should we subjects of the Japanese Empire now take toward the various problems of the day? It seems to us that our first duty is the task of creating a new Japanese culture by sublimating and assimilating foreign cultures which are at the source of the various problems in keeping with the fundamental principles of our national entity.

Every type of foreign ideology that has been imported into our country may have been quite natural in China, India, Europe, or America, in that it has sprung from their racial or historical characteristics; but in our country, which has a unique national entity, it is necessary as a preliminary step to put these types to rigid judgment and scrutiny so as to see if they are suitable to our national traits. That is to say, the creation of a new culture which has characteristics peculiar to our nation can be looked forward to only through this consciousness and the sublimation and assimilation of foreign cultures that accompanies it. . . .

To put it in a nutshell, while the strong points of Occidental learning and concepts lie in their analytical and intellectual qualities, the characteristics of Oriental learning and concepts lie in their intuitive and ascetic qualities. These are natural tendencies that arise through racial and historical differences; and when we compare them with our national spirit, concepts, or mode of living, we cannot help recognizing further great and fundamental differences. Our nation has in the past imported, assimilated, and sublimated Chinese and Indian ideologies, and has therewith supported the Imperial Way, making possible the establishment of an original culture based on her national entity. Following the Meiji Restoration Occidental cultures poured in with a rush, and contributed immensely toward our national prosperity; but their individualistic qualities brought about various difficulties in all the phases of the lives of our people, causing their thoughts to fluctuate. However, now is the time for us to sublimate and assimilate these Occidental ideologies in keeping with our national entity, to set up a vast new Japanese culture, and, by taking advantage of these things, to bring about a great national development.

7

Post–World War II (1945–present)

Among the many postwar developments, the forced dismantling of State Shinto stands out as a decisive event. The Allies not only occupied Japan for a time, they also demanded the adoption of a new constitution that emphasized the separation of church and state. Article 89 of the new constitution states that "no public money or other property shall be expended ... for benefit or maintenance of any religious institution or association." They also believed it important that the emperor renounce his divine status as a living kami descended from Amaterasu. According to Harold G. Henderson, a Lieutenant Colonel in the United States Army, an Englishman (named R.H. Blyth) employed by both the United States and the Imperial Household floated this idea with the Japanese and reported that the Emperor was "not only willing but anxious to renounce his 'divinity'" ... and "that he did not believe in it himself." The Allies were, of course, delighted to hear this because they were not particularly looking forward to confronting the Japanese on this issue. Blyth wrote the first draft of the rescript reprinted below.*

7.1 THE END OF STATE SHINTO

Many Japanese intellectuals as well as the Allied military leaders believed that Shinto had during the prewar period been used by the Japanese military to support the war effort. Therefore, it seemed important to prevent this from happening again by stopping whatever special privileges Shinto, especially State Shinto, enjoyed.

After the dismantling of State Shinto, the semi-free religious market that developed during the Meiji Restoration expanded and many new religious movements developed as they competed for private donations and new adherents. No longer did State Shinto enjoy financial support from public monies. Some predicted the demise of all forms of Shinto, but Shrine Shinto managed to transform itself into what we might call a denomination. In 1946, the Association of Shinto Shrines came into being and many of the diverse local shrines became affiliated with each other.

The fate of Shinto in postwar Japan and the actions of the Japanese government must be considered in light of the horror of the two atomic bombs that were dropped on Nagasaki and Hiroshima. The world had never before witnessed such devastation and massive loss of life in such a short period of time. The shame experienced by defeat was compounded by the death, destruction, and pollution these bombs unleashed.

Two documents follow. The first is the directive that dismantled State Shinto and the second is an Imperial Rescript, which declares, among other things, that the emperor has no special divine status. These documents are particularly interesting in light of the instructions found in the Joint Army-Navy Manual of Military Government and Civil Affairs (November 4, 1943) para. 9m, p. 19, which states: "International law requires that religious convictions and practices be respected. Therefore, places of religious worship should not be closed unless as a security or sanitary measure."

---

*See Appendix E:4 and E:5 of William P. Woodard, *The Allied Occupation of Japan 1945–1952 and Japanese Religions* (Leiden: E. J. Brill, 1972), 317–319.

[Directive for the] Abolition of Governmental Sponsorship, Support, Perpetuation, Control, and Dissemination of State Shinto

READING QUESTIONS

1. What are the goals of this directive?
2. How does the directive propose to accomplish these goals?
3. How does the directive propose to deal with State Shinto, Sect Shinto, and Shrine Shinto?
4. Do you think it is appropriate for nations that conquer other nations to require them to change their laws regulating religion? Why or why not?

SCAPIN 448 (CIE) 15 DEC 45 (AG 000.3)

1. In order to free the Japanese people from direct or indirect compulsion to believe or profess to believe in a religion or cult officially designated by the state, and

    In order to lift from the Japanese people the burden of compulsory financial support of an ideology which has contributed to their war guilt, defeat, suffering, privation, and present deplorable condition, and

    In order to prevent a recurrence of the perversion of Shinto theory and beliefs into militaristic and ultranationalistic propaganda designed to delude the Japanese people and lead them into wars of aggression, and

    In order to assist the Japanese people in a rededication of their national life to building a

new Japan based upon ideals of perpetual peace and democracy,

    It is hereby directed that:

a. The sponsorship, support, perpetuation, control and dissemination of Shinto by the Japanese national, prefectural, and local governments, or by public officials, subordinates, and employees acting in their official capacity are prohibited and will cease immediately.

b. All financial support from public funds and all official affiliation with Shinto and Shinto shrines are prohibited and will cease immediately.

    (1) While no financial support from public funds will be extended to shrines located on public reservations or parks, this prohibition will not be construed to preclude the Japanese Government from continuing to support the areas on which such shrines are located.

    (2) Private financial support of all Shinto shrines which have been previously supported in whole or in part by public funds will be permitted, provided such private support is entirely voluntary and is in no way derived from forced or involuntary contributions.

c. All propagation and dissemination of militaristic and ultra-nationalistic ideology in Shinto doctrines, practices, rites, ceremonies, or observances, as well as in the doctrines, practices, rites, ceremonies, and observances of any other religion, faith, sect, creed, or philosophy, are prohibited and will cease immediately.

d. The Religious Functions Order relating to the Grand Shrine of Ise and the Religious Functions Order relating to State and other Shrines will be annulled.

e. The Shrine Board (*Jingi-in*) of the Ministry of Home Affairs will be abolished, and its present functions, duties, and administrative obligations will not be assumed by any other governmental or tax-supported agency.

f. All public educational institutions whose primary function is either the investigation and dissemination of Shinto or the training of a Shinto priesthood will be abolished and their physical properties diverted to other uses. Their present functions, duties and administrative obligations will not be

From the Civil Affairs Division of the War Department, Washington, D.C.—Supreme Commander of Allied Powers Instructions (directive) #448, Civil Information and Education Section, 15 Dec. 45 (AG 000.3). A copy of this directive can be found in Appendix B:5 of William P. Woodard, *The Allied Occupation of Japan 1945–1952 and Japanese Religions.* (Leiden: E. J. Brill, 1972), 295–298.

assumed by any other governmental or tax-supported agency.

g. Private educational institutions for the investigation and dissemination of Shinto and for the training of priesthood for Shinto will be permitted and will operate with the same privileges and be subject to the same controls and restrictions as any other private educational institution having no affiliation with the government; in no case, however, will they receive support from public funds, and in no case will they propagate and disseminate militaristic and ultra-nationalistic ideology.

h. The dissemination of Shinto doctrines in any form and by any means in any educational institution supported wholly or in part by public funds is prohibited and will cease immediately.

    (1) All teachers' manuals and textbooks now in use in any educational institution supported wholly or in part by public funds will be censored, and all Shinto doctrine will be deleted. No teachers' manual or textbook which is published in the future for use in such institutions will contain any Shinto doctrine.

    (2) No visits to Shinto shrines and no rites, practices or ceremonies associated with Shinto will be conducted or sponsored by any educational institution supported wholly or in part by public funds.

i. Circulation by the government of "The Fundamental Principles of the National Structure" (*Kokutai no Hongi*), "The Way of the Subject' (*Shinmin no Michi*), and all similar official volumes, commentaries, interpretations, or instructions on Shinto is prohibited.

j. The use in official writings of the terms "Greater East Asia War" (*Dai Tōa Sensō*), "The Whole World under One Roof" (*Hakko Ichi-u*), and all other terms whose connotation in Japanese is inextricably connected with State Shinto, militarism, and ultranationalism is prohibited and will cease immediately.

k. God-shelves (*Kamidana*) and all other physical symbols of State Shinto in any office, school, institution, organization, or structure supported wholly or in part by public funds are prohibited and will be removed immediately.

l. No official, subordinate, employee, student, citizen, or resident of Japan will be discriminated against because of his failure to profess and believe in or participate in any practice, rite, ceremony, or observance of State Shinto or of any other religion.

m. No official of the national, prefectural, or local government, acting in his public capacity, will visit any shrine to report his assumption of office, to report on conditions of government or to participate as a representative of government in any ceremony or observance.

2. a. The purpose of this directive is to separate religion from the state, to prevent misuse of religion for political ends, and to put all religions, faiths, and creeds upon exactly the same basis, entitled to precisely the same opportunities and protection. It forbids affiliation with the government and the propagation and dissemination of militaristic and ultra-nationalistic ideology not only to Shinto but to the followers of all religions, faiths, sects, creeds, or philosophies.

b. The provisions of this directive will apply with equal force to all rites, practices, ceremonies, observances, beliefs, teachings, mythology, legends, philosophy, shrines, and physical symbols associated with Shinto.

c. The term State Shinto within the meaning of this directive will refer to that branch of Shinto (*Kokka Shintō or Jinja Shintō*) which by official acts of the Japanese Government has been differentiated from the religion of Sect Shinto (*Shūha Shintō or Kyōha Shintō*) and has been classified a nonreligious cult commonly known as State Shinto, National Shinto, or Shrine Shinto.

d. The term Sect Shinto (*Shūha Shintō* or *Kyōha Shintō*) will refer to that branch of Shinto (composed of 13 recognized sects) which by popular belief, legal commentary, and the official acts of the Japanese Government has been recognized to be a religion.

e. Pursuant to the terms of Article I of the Basic Directive on "Removal of Restrictions on Political, Civil, and Religious Liberties" issued on 4 October 1945 by the Supreme Commander for the Allied Powers in which the Japanese people were assured complete religious freedom,

(1) Sect Shinto will enjoy the same protection as any other religion.

(2) Shrine Shinto, after having been divorced from the state and divested of its militaristic and ultranationalistic elements, will be recognized as a religion if its adherents so desire and will be granted the same protection as any other religion in so far as it may in fact be the philosophy or religion of Japanese individuals.

f. Militaristic and ultra-nationalistic ideology, as used in this directive, embraces those teachings, beliefs, and theories which advocate or justify a mission on the part of Japan to extend its rule over other nations and peoples by reason of:

(1) The doctrine that the Emperor of Japan is superior to the heads of other states because of ancestry, descent, or special origin.

(2) The doctrine that the people of Japan are superior to the people of other lands because of ancestry, descent, or special origin.

(3) The doctrine that the islands of Japan are superior to other lands because of divine or special origin.

(4) Any other doctrine which tends to delude the Japanese people into embarking upon wars of aggression or to glorify the use of force as an instrument for the settlement of disputes with other peoples.

3. The Imperial Japanese Government will submit a comprehensive report to this Headquarters not later than 15 March 1946 describing in detail all action taken to comply with all provisions of this directive.

4. All officials, subordinates, and employees of the Japanese national, prefectural, and local governments, all teachers and education officials, and all citizens and residents of Japan will be held personally accountable for compliance with the spirit as well as the letter of all provisions of this directive.

Imperial Rescript of January 1, 1946

READING QUESTIONS

1. In your opinion, what is the most important part of the *Imperial Rescript?* Why do you deem it important?
2. What is the religious significance of the *Imperial Rescript?*

In greeting the New Year, We recall to mind that Emperor Meiji proclaimed, as the basis of our national policy, the Five Clauses of the Charter Oath at the beginning of the Meiji Era. The Charter Oath signified:

1. Deliberative assemblies shall be established and all measures of government decided in accordance with public opinion.
2. All classes, high and low, shall unite in vigorously carrying on the affairs of State.
3. All common people, no less than the civil and military officials, shall be allowed to fulfill their just desires, so that there may not be any discontent among them.
4. All the absurd usages of old shall be broken through, and equity and justice to be found in the workings of nature shall serve as the basis of action.
5. Wisdom and knowledge shall be sought throughout the world for the purpose of promoting the welfare of the Empire.

The proclamation is evident in significance and high in its ideals. We wish to make this oath anew and restore the country to stand on its own feet again. We have to reaffirm the principles embodied in the Charter, and proceed unflinchingly towards elimination of misguided practices of the past, and keeping in close touch with the

---

This official document from the Japanese government can be found in Appendix E:3 of William P. Woodard, *The Allied Occupation of Japan 1945–1952 and Japanese Religions* (Leiden: E. J. Brill, 1972), 315–316. Footnote omitted.

desires of the people, we will construct a new Japan through thoroughly being pacific, the officials and the people alike, attaining rich culture, and advancing the standard of living of the people.

The devastation of war inflicted upon our cities, the miseries of the destitute, the stagnation of trade, shortage of food, and the great and growing number of the unemployed are indeed heart-rending. But if the nation is firmly united in its resolve to face the present ordeal and to seek civilization consistently in peace, a bright future will undoubtedly be ours, not only for our country, but for the whole humanity.

Love of the family and love of the country are especially strong in this country. With more of this devotion should we now work towards love of mankind.

We feel deeply concerned to note that consequent upon the protracted war ending in our defeat, our people are liable to grow restless and to fall into the Slough of Despond. Radical tendencies in excess are gradually spreading and the sense of morality tends to lose its hold on the people, with the result that there are signs of confusion of thoughts.

We stand by the people and We wish always to share with them in their moments of joys and sorrows. The ties between Us and Our people have always stood upon mutual trust and affection. They do not depend upon mere legends and myths. They are not predicated on the false conception that the Emperor is divine, and that the Japanese people are superior to other races and fated to rule the world.

Our Government should make every effort to alleviate their trials and tribulations. At the same time, We trust that the people will rise to the occasion, and will strive courageously for the solution of their outstanding difficulties, and for the development of industry and culture. Acting upon a consciousness of solidarity and of mutual aid and broad tolerance in their civic life, they will prove themselves worthy of their best tradition. By their supreme endeavours in that direction, they will be able to render their substantial contribution to the welfare and advancement of mankind.

The resolution for the year should be made at the beginning of the year. We expect Our people to join Us in all exertions looking to accomplishment of this great undertaking with an indomitable spirit.

7.2 THE HONORED DEAD

It is one thing to announce formally and legally the separation of church and state; it is another to disentangle religion from the public life of a nation. One controversy that arose from the effort to separate church and state in Japan concerned the question of whether or not the Yasukuni Shrine, a Shinto shrine that memorializes the war dead, should receive public support.

Shinto, with its concern for honoring ancestors, was a natural vehicle for creating rituals and shrines to commemorate those fallen in battle. The Yasukuni Shrine was established in 1869 by the Emperor Meiji to enshrine and honor the spirits of those who died in the Boshin War (1868–1869), which resulted in the restoration of imperial power after the collapse of the shogunate. It continued to be important through World War II but when the new Japanese constitution was adopted after the war, the shrine lost state support and became a private religious organization.

Today, the Yasukuni Shrine has become a site of contention. The Association of Bereaved Families along with Japanese political conservatives have demanded the shrine receive state support as a war memorial. Those on the political left along with Christians have argued that the shrine is more than a war memorial, that it is a Shinto shrine and hence religious. Therefore, it should not receive state support. The extent of the controversy has spread beyond Japan's borders, and in 1985 when Prime Minister Nakasone paid an official visit to the shrine, China and other nations that suffered at the hands of the Japanese during World War II lodged strong protests.

Today the shrine remains private and, as those with living memories of the war dead pass on, it has attempted to convey to a new generation a sense of respect for the men and women lost in the war. The following is a guide to the Yasukuni shrine for children.

TRANSLATED BY RICHARD GARDNER

A [Child's] Guide to Yasukuni Shrine: Our Yasukuni Shrine

READING QUESTIONS

1. Do you find it ironic that a shrine dedicated to the war dead should have over six hundred white pigeons symbolizing peace? Can you think of parallels in other countries that combine the memorializing of war dead with symbols of peace?
2. What is it the authors of this guide are hoping to get the children to believe about the recent military history of Japan?
3. Is there a significant difference between worshiping the soldiers killed in war as kami and honoring soldiers as heroes that you find in other countries? If so, what is it?

Dear Fathers and Mothers:

The whole family can have an intimate visit with the gods by worshipping at the inner sanctuary of the Main Sanctuary. Please feel free to make an application at the reception office. We also look forward to welcoming your visit on days of celebration such as Coming of Age Day, the Children's Festival, and the First Visit of Newborns to the Shrine.

THE CHERRY TREES OF YASUKUNI

At the time of the construction of the Main Sanctuary of Yasukuni Shrine in Meiji 3 (1870), Someiyoshino cherry trees were planted within the shrine grounds. This was the beginning of the cherry trees of Yasukuni. The graceful, beautiful cherry trees of Kudan, which all the gods are very proud of, are a symbol of Yasukuni Shrine. At present there are about a thousand cherry trees—including Someiyoshino, mountain cherry, and others—within the shrine gardens. As spring approaches every year, the Meteorological Agency examines the Someiyoshino at Yasukuni in order to predict when the cherry trees will bloom in Tokyo.

From *Religions of Japan in Practice*, edited by George J. Tanabe, Jr., translated by Richard Gardner. Copyright © 1999 by Princeton University Press. Reprinted by permission of Princeton University Press.

THE WHITE PIGEONS OF YASUKUNI

There are about six hundred of Poppo the Pigeon's friends here. They are all pure white carrier pigeons [*hato*, which also means dove, the symbol of peace], a type born only once every ten thousand births. Twice every day Leopold Mozart's "Toy Symphony" wafts throughout the grounds to tell Poppo and his friends that it is time to dine.

POPPO THE WISE PIGEON'S "ANSWERS TO ANY AND ALL QUESTIONS ABOUT YASUKUNI"

POPPO: Good day everyone! I'm Poppo the White Pigeon. There are about six hundred of my friends living together peacefully here at Yasukuni. We've come to be great friends with everyone looking after and visiting the shrine and are always having fun playing about the shrine grounds. So if it is something to do with Yasukuni, we know every nook and cranny of the place. Let's talk a bit about the history and festivals of Yasukuni Shrine, which everyone is always asking about.

Q: Who built Yasukuni Shrine and when?

A: Yasukuni Shrine is a shrine with a long tradition and was built over 120 years ago in 1869. Throughout the time of national seclusion before the Meiji period, Japan did not have relations with the other countries of the world. But the people of foreign countries gradually took a critical attitude toward Japan and pressured Japan to open itself to the outside world.

Wondering "what in the world should we do," the whole country was in an uproar and public opinion was widely split between those wanting to open the country and those wanting to keep it closed. In this situation, the Tokugawa Bakufu, which had been entrusted with the governing of Japan for over three hundred years, lost the power to quell this disturbance and so returned the authority to govern to the emperor.

At this point was born the idea of everyone in Japan becoming of one heart and mind under the emperor in order to restore the beautiful traditions of Japan, create a splendid modern nation, and become good friends with all the people of the world.

Then in the midst of trying to achieve this great rebirth, the Boshin War—an unfortunate, internal dispute—occurred, and many people came forth to offer their lives for the country. In order to transmit to future ages the story of the people who died in the Meiji Restoration, which aimed at creating a new age, the

Emperor Meiji built this shrine, then named Tokyo Shokonsha (Shrine for Summoning the Spirits), here at Kudan in Tokyo in the sixth month of 1869. In 1879 the name was changed to Yasukuni Shrine.

Q: What does "Yasukuni" mean?

A: The Honorable Shrine Name "Yasukuni Shrine" was bestowed on the shrine by Emperor Meiji. The "Yasukuni" in the name means "Let's make our country a place of tranquility and gentle peace, an always peaceful country" and reflects the great and noble feelings of the Emperor Meiji. All the gods who are worshipped at the Yasukuni Shrine gave their noble lives in order to protect Japan while praying for eternal peace, like the Emperor Meiji, from the depths of their heart.

Q: What gods are worshipped at Yasukuni Shrine?

A: I explained a bit about the Boshin War earlier. The over 3,500 pillars (when counting gods, we count not "one, two" but "one pillar, two pillars") who died at that time were the first gods worshipped here. Later, all of those who died devoting themselves to the country, from 1853 (the year the American Admiral Perry led four warships to Uragaoki in Kanagawa Prefecture and everyone was saying with shock, "Black ships have come!") to the end of the Bakufu fifteen years later, were also enshrined and worshipped here.

After that there were also numerous battles within the country—such as those of the Saga Disturbance and the Seinan War [both of which were revolts against the newly established Meiji government]—until the new Japan was firmly established. All those who died for their country in those battles are also worshipped here. Everyone's ancestors helped carry out the important mission of creating a marvelous Japan with the emperor at its center.

However, to protect the independence of Japan and the peace of Asia surrounding Japan, there were also—though it is a very sad thing—several wars with foreign countries. In the Meiji period there were the Sino-Japanese War and the Russian-Japanese War; in the Taishō period, the First World War; and in the Shōwa period, the Manchurian Incident, the China Incident, and then the Great Pacific War (the Second World War).

At the start of the Russian-Japanese War, Emperor Meiji expressed his deep sorrow by composing and reciting an August Poem: "Though all are linked like the waters of the four seas, why do storms arise in the world?" (Why does peace give way to the storms of war when all the countries of the world should be like brothers?)

War is truly a sorrowful thing. But it was necessary to fight to firmly protect the independence of Japan and to exist as a peaceful nation prospering together with the surrounding countries of Asia. All those who offered up their noble lives in such disturbances and wars are worshipped at Yasukuni Shrine as gods.

Q: Could you please teach us some more about the gods?

A: Do you all know how many gods there are at Yasukuni Shrine? The answer is over 2,467,000! There are this many gods in front of all of you who have come to worship here! Let me tell you a little about the gods.

Among the gods at Yasukuni Shrine, there are gods such as Hashimoto Sanai [1834–1859], Yoshida Shōin [1830–1859], Sakamoto Ryōma [1836–1867], and Takasugi Shinsaku [1839–1867], who you all know well from history books and television dramas and who worked hard for the country from the end of the Edo period to the beginning of the Meiji period [by opposing the shogunate and supporting the emperor]. Also worshipped here are the many soldiers who died in battle during the wars of the Meiji, Taishō, and Shōwa periods.

But there are not just soldiers here; there are also over fifty-seven thousand female gods here. There are also children like you, and even younger, who are worshipped here as gods.

Let me tell you a little about the Great Pacific War, which took place over fifty years ago. When the American Army attacked Okinawa, there were junior high school students who stood up and resisted with the soldiers. To defend Okinawa and their hometowns, over sixteen hundred boys of nine schools—Okinawa Shihan School, the Number One and Number Two Prefectural Junior High Schools, etc.—formed groups such as the Blood and Iron Imperial Brigade and fought just like soldiers. Also, over four hundred students of girls schools, such as Number One Prefectural Girls High School, Number Two Prefectural Girls High School, and Shuri Girls High School, served as nurses on the battlefield or made their way through the battlefield carrying food and ammunition. Most of those boy and girl students fell in battle. Now they are enshrined in Yasukuni Shrine and are sleeping here peacefully.

There are also fifteen hundred who met their sad end when the *Tsushima Maru* transport ship, which was evacuating them from Okinawa to Kagoshima to escape the bombing, was hit by torpedoes from enemy submarines. Among them were seven hundred grade school children.

There are also many, just like your older brothers and older sisters, who died in bombing attacks when they gave up their studies because of the war and worked hard producing goods in factories.

The next story is something that happened on August 20, 1945. Though the war was already over, the Soviet Army suddenly attacked Karafuto (now Sakhalin). The girl telephone operators of Maoka in Karafuto continued reporting the movements of the Soviet Army to the mainland as the enemy approached. Their last message before losing their lives was, "Farewell everybody, this is the end, sayonara." All of them are here.

Also among the gods here are many who fell leading the fight to put out the fires caused by enemy bombing attacks on Japan. Nurses attached to the army on the battlefield who bore the noble insignia of the Red Cross and were adored like a mother or older sister. The crews of military transport ships who one and all sank to the bottom of the sea while heading to the southern battle-front. Cameramen and newspaper reporters attached to the army who fell from enemy bullets while gathering stories on the battlefield. Many people like this are worshipped here with great devotion as noble, godly spirits who gave their lives for their homeland Japan.

There are also those here who took the responsibility for the war upon themselves and ended their own lives when the Great Pacific War ended. There are also 1,068 who had their lives cruelly taken after the war when they were falsely and one-sidedly branded as "war criminals" by the kangaroo court of the Allies who had fought Japan. At Yasukuni Shrine we call these the "Shōwa Martyrs" [including General Tōjō Hideki], and they are all worshipped as gods.

YASUKUNI SHRINE IS THE SHRINE WHERE ALL JAPANESE GO TO WORSHIP

So now you know what gods are worshipped at Yasukuni Shrine. The gods of Yasukuni Shrine gave their noble lives on the battlefield with the hope that Japan might continue forever in peace and independence and that the marvelous history and traditions of Japan bequeathed by our ancestors might continue on and on forever. That Japan is peaceful and prosperous is thanks to all of those who have become gods at Yasukuni Shrine. From now on you must treasure "Our Japan," which these people protected by giving their lives in times of war. So let's all come to worship at Yasukuni Shrine, offer up our feelings of thanks to the gods, and promise to become splendid people. Flying above the shrine grounds, all us pigeons will be looking forward to your coming to worship.

7.3 MARRIAGE

The Japanese believe that contact with the dead "pollutes" a person, so most funerals are conducted by Buddhist not Shinto priests. However, marriage is

not polluting. It is a celebration of union, fertility, and the continuation of the family. With the emphasis on the fertility of nature and the value of the ancestral line found in tradition Shinto, it seems only natural for Shinto priests to conduct marriage ceremonies. Marriage is a rite of passage and the religious rites surrounding it mark an important transition point on the journey of life.

There was no standardized Shinto wedding ceremony until 1900. Even today priests at different shrines compose their own ceremonies that incorporate local elements, although there is more standardization than in the past. What follows is a typical *norito* or liturgy that is used today. It marks the transition to a new life, yet it incorporates past tradition reminding those who are about to be wed that they are participating in something larger than their own private pledge of love. This *norito* is a translation of a wedding ceremony composed by the head priest at the Hawaii Daijingu Shrine.

TRANSLATED BY CHERISH PRATT

The Shinto Wedding Text: A Modern Norito

READING QUESTIONS

1. What similarities and what differences do you note between this ceremonial wedding text and wedding ceremonies that you have witnessed?
2. What important social functions do you think this wedding ceremony reinforces?
3. How is this *norito* related to traditional Shinto mythology?

We humbly speak before the Majestic and Sovereign
Deity, who is awe inspiring and most highly
revered.
We imitate the work of the deities who performed this
in days of old.

Under the auspices of the go-between [*insert name*],
who by grasping the middle of the majestic spear
bids the bride [*insert woman's name*] and groom [*insert
man's name*] make a wedding vow.

This day has been designated for ritual.
Due to its auspicious character we celebrate the
wedding ceremony today.

It is because the law of marriage is majestically carried
out in front of the great deities that the proper
deportment of ritual must follow.
We make offerings of Sacred Food and Sacred Sake;
A variety of tastes are here arranged and set before
you.
Eat with delight, listen to the aroma of the offerings,
enjoy, and so accept.

The exchange of sake, three times drunk, shared, and
poured for each other.

We do that because we are extending our
congratulations to each other.
The vow does not exhaust itself; the cup is never dry.

The Vows we articulate are intricately inlaid into our
lives in this world and the next.
Growing old together, until our hair is long and white,
we have been caused to be tied.
So does our bond exist in the universe,
just as the sun and moon exist in the heavens
just as the mountains and rivers exist on earth.
Side by side, shoulder to shoulder, putting our home,
the *ie*, in order, making it settled.

Maintain the family gate as a dignified one.
The connection to the ancestors is to be continued and
not neglected.
The family name should flourish, be highly respected
and widely known.

Our grandchildren and grandchildren should continue
forever,
just as the fifty red oak trees, just as the eight
mulberry bushes prosper and propagate.

Thus we humbly and most respectfully speak.

8

So What Is Shinto?

Kuroda Toshio (1926–1993), a postwar scholar of medieval Japanese history, provided a revisionist history of Shinto. According to Kuroda, Shinto was not an independent religion until modern times. Contrary to standard claims, what we call Shinto today is not the indigenous religion of Japan. Kuroda thinks that the beliefs and practices usually associated with Shinto were part of a larger worldview that included Buddhism and other elements. If so, the distinction between that which constitutes foreign imports and indigenous factors breaks down.

In the following essay, Kuroda pays close attention to how the term *Shinto* has been used in ancient documents. He concludes that the word has been used in a variety of ways and only in modern times does it assume a meaning that indicates some kind of distinct, indigenous Japanese religion.

KURODA TOSHIO

Shinto in the History of Japanese Religion

READING QUESTIONS

1. What are the two general categories into which discussions of the role of Shinto in Japanese history divide?
2. What does Kuroda hope to demonstrate?

From *Religions of Japan in Practice*, edited by George J. Tanabe, Jr., translated by James C. Dobbins and Suzanne Gay. Copyright © 1999 by Princeton University Press. Reprinted by permission of Princeton University Press.

3. What does Kuroda conclude from his study of the word *Shinto* in the *Nihon shoki*?
4. When did the notion of Shinto as Japan's indigenous religion finally emerge?
5. What do you think the author means when he says, " . . . while acquiring independence, Shinto declined to the state of a religion that disavowed being a religion"?

Shintō has long been regarded as a crucial element in Japanese religion that gives it distinctiveness and individuality. The common person's view of Shintō usually includes the following assumptions: Shintō bears the unmistakable characteristics of a primitive religion, including nature worship and taboos against *kegare* (impurities), but it has no system of doctrine; it exists in diverse forms as folk belief but at the same time possesses certain features of organized religion—for example, rituals and institutions such as shrines; it also plays an important role in Japan's ancient mythology and provides a basis for ancestor and emperor worship. In short, Shintō is viewed as the indigenous religion of Japan, continuing in an unbroken line from prehistoric times down to the present.

Many people have discussed the role of Shintō in Japanese history and culture, but depending on the person there are slight differences in interpretation. These can be divided into two general categories. The first includes those who believe that, despite the dissemination of Buddhism and Confucianism, the religion called Shintō has existed without interruption throughout Japanese history. This has become the common person's view, and it is the conviction of Shintō scholars and priests particularly. The second includes those who think that, aside from whether it existed under the name Shintō, throughout history there have always been Shintōlike beliefs and customs (*shinkō*). This kind of interpretation is frequently found in studies of Japanese culture or intellectual history. This view can be traced back to the National Learning (*kokugaku*) scholar

Motoori Norinaga in the eighteenth century, and it is reflected more recently in Yanagida Kunio's work on Japanese folklore. The same trend is discernible in the writings of Hori Ichirō, who claims an opinion similar to Robert Bellah's and Sir Charles Eliot's. Hori defines Shintō and "Shintōness" as "the underlying will of Japanese culture." He argues that Shintō has been the crucial element bringing the "great mix" of religions and rituals absorbed by the Japanese people into coexistence. Moreover, it has forced them to become Japanese in character. Maruyama Masao, speaking as an intellectual historian on the historical consciousness of the Japanese people, is also of this school. He maintains that the thought processes found in the myths of the *Kojiki* and the *Nihon shoki* continue to exist as an "ancient stratum," even though other layers of thought have been superimposed in subsequent ages. Maruyama is somewhat sympathetic to "Shintō thinkers of the Edo period"—including of course Motoori Norinaga—"down to the nationalistic moralists of the 1930s," and he even construes their assertions to be "a truth born of a certain kind of intuition."

Of these two groups, the views of the second demand special attention, but they should not be looked upon separately from those of the first. The two represent in a sense the external and the internal aspects of the same phenomenon. The views of the second group can be summarized as follows:

1. Shintō, with the Japanese people, is enduring. It is "the underlying will of Japanese culture," to borrow Hori Ichirō's phrase, an underlying autonomy that transforms and assimilates diverse cultural elements imported from outside. In the words of Motoori, any cultural element of any period (even Buddhism and Confucianism) is, "broadly speaking, the Shintō of that period."

2. Even though one can speak of Shintō as a religion along with Buddhism and Taoism, "Shintōness" is something deeper. It is the cultural will or energy of the Japanese people, embodied in conventions that precede or transcend religion. Here, the "secularity of Shintō" is stressed. Whether people who maintain this position like it or not, what they advocate is akin to the Meiji Constitution, which did not regard State Shintō as a religion and on that basis placed restraints upon the thought and beliefs of Japanese citizens. It is also similar to the rationale adopted by certain movements today that seek to revive State Shintō.

3. Based on this line of thought, "the miscellaneous nature of Japanese religion," whereby a person may be Buddhist and Shintō at the same time, is taken as an unchanging characteristic of Japanese culture. When such a formula is applied to all cultural phenomena in history, then a miscellaneous, expedient, irrational, and nonintellectual frame of mind, more than any effort at a logical, unified, and integrated worldview, is extolled as that which is most Japanese.

The views of the second group when compared to those of the first differ in conception and central argument, but insofar as they both regard Shintō as a unique religion existing independently throughout history, the two share a common premise and reinforce one another. This view, however, is not only an incorrect perception of the facts but also a one-sided interpretation of Japanese history and culture. It is hoped that this article will demonstrate that before modern times Shintō did not exist as an independent religion. The main points of my argument will be as follows:

1. It is generally held that an indigenous self-consciousness is embodied in the word Shintō. I would argue that the original meaning of the word differs from how it is understood today.

2. The ceremonies of Ise Shrine, as well as those of the imperial court and the early provincial government, are said to have been forms of "pure Shintō." I would like to show that they actually became one component of a unique system of Buddhism that emerged in Japan and were perceived as an extension of Buddhism.

3. It is said that Shintō played a secular role in society and existed in a completely different sphere from Buddhism. I would maintain that this very secularity was permeated with Buddhist concepts and was itself religious in nature. The greater part of this paper will examine this question and the preceding two in their ancient and medieval contexts.

4. Finally, I would like to trace the historical stages and the rationale whereby the term Shintō came to mean the indigenous religion or national faith of Japan and to clarify how and when Shintō came to be viewed as an independent religion.

SHINTŌ IN THE *NIHON SHOKI*

The word Shintō is commonly taken to mean Japan's indigenous religion and to have had that meaning from fairly early times. It is difficult, however, to find a clear-cut example of the word Shintō used in such a way in early writings. The intellectual historian Tsuda Sōkichi has studied the occurrences of the word Shintō in early Japanese literature and has divided its meaning into the following six categories: (1) "religious beliefs found in indigenous customs passed down in Japan, including superstitious beliefs"; (2) "the authority, power, activity, or deeds of a kami, the status of kami, being kami, or the kami itself"; (3) concepts and teachings concerning kami; (4) the teachings propagated by a particular shrine; (5) "the way of the kami" as a political or moral norm; and (6) sectarian Shintō as found in new religions. From these it is clear that the word Shintō has been used in a great variety of ways. Tsuda maintains that in the *Nihon shoki* Shintō means "the religious beliefs found in indigenous customs in Japan," the first definition, and that it was used from that time to distinguish "Japan's indigenous religion from Buddhism." He also claims that this basic definition underlies the meaning of Shintō in the other five categories.

It is far from conclusive, however, that the word Shintō was used in early times to denote Japan's indigenous religion, and for that reason Tsuda's analysis of examples in the *Nihon shoki* should be reexamined. The following three sentences are the only instances of the word Shintō in the *Nihon shoki*:

1. The emperor believed in the teachings of the Buddha (*Buppō* or *Hotoke no minori*) and revered Shintō (or *kami no michi*). (Prologue on Emperor Yōmei)

2. The emperor revered the teachings of the Buddha but scorned Shintō. He cut down the trees at Ikukunitama Shrine. (Prologue on Emperor Kōtoku)

3. The expression "as a kami would" (*kamunagara*) means to conform to Shintō. It also means in essence to possess one's self of Shintō. (Entry for Taika 3/4/26)

In examples 1 and 2 it is possible to interpret Shintō as distinguishing "Japan's indigenous religion from Buddhism," but that need not be the only interpretation. Tsuda himself indicates that in China the word Shintō originally meant various folk religions, or Taoism, or sometimes Buddhism, or even religion in general. Therefore, the word Shintō is actually a generic term for popular beliefs, whether of China, Korea, or Japan, even though in examples 1 and 2 it refers specifically to Japan's ancient customs, rituals, and beliefs, regardless of whether they were Japanese in origin. Since the *Nihon shoki* was compiled with a knowledge of China in mind, it is hard to imagine that its author used the Chinese word Shintō solely to mean Japan's indigenous religion. Though there may be some validity in what Tsuda says, the word Shintō by itself probably means popular beliefs in general.

In examples 1 and 2 Shintō is used in contrast to the word *Buppō*, the teachings of the Buddha. Tsuda takes this to mean "Japan's indigenous religion," but there are other possible interpretations of this without construing it to be the name of a religion. For example, it could mean "the authority, power, activity, or deeds of a kami, the status of kami, being a kami, or the kami itself," Tsuda's second definition of Shintō. In fact, during this period the character *dō* or *tō*, which is found in the word Shintō, meant not so much road or path but rather conduct or right action. Hence, Shintō could easily refer to the conduct or action of the kami.

In example 3 there are two instances of the word Shintō. While it is not unthinkable to interpret them as "popular beliefs in general," Tsuda's second definition, "the authority, power, activity, or deeds of a kami," is perhaps more appropriate, since the word *kamunagara* in the quotation means "in the nature of a kami" or "in the state of being a kami." The sentences in example 3 were originally a note explaining the word *kamunagara* as it appeared in the emperor's decree issued on the day of this entry, and according to Edo period scholars it was added sometime after the ninth century when the work was transcribed. Therefore, it is not reliable as evidence for what Shintō meant at the time the *Nihon shoki* was compiled. Even if it were, it is more likely that the compiler did not use the same word in two different ways but rather applied the same definition, "the authority, power, activity, or deeds of a kami," in all three examples.

Another possible interpretation of Shintō in the *Nihon shoki* is Taoism. Based on recent studies, it is clear that Shintō was another term for Taoism in China during the same period. Moreover, as Taoist concepts and practices steadily passed into Japan between the first century A.D. and the period when the *Nihon shoki* was compiled, they no doubt exerted a considerable influence on the ceremonies and the beliefs of communal groups bound by blood ties or geographical proximity and on those that emerged around imperial authority. Among the many elements of Taoist origin transmitted to Japan are the following: veneration of swords and mirrors as religious symbols; titles such as *mahito* or *shinjin* (Taoist meaning—perfected man, Japanese meaning—the highest of eight court ranks in ancient times which the emperor bestowed on his descendants), *hijiri* or *sen* (Taoist—immortal, Japanese—saint, emperor, or recluse), and *tennō* (Taoist—lord of the universe, Japanese—emperor); the cults of Polaris and the Big Dipper; terms associated with Ise Shrine such as *jingū* (Taoist—a hall enshrining a deity, Japanese—Ise Shrine), *naikū* (Chinese—inner palace, Japanese—Inner Shrine at Ise), *gekū* (Chinese—detached palace, Japanese—Outer Shrine at Ise), and *taiichi* (Taoist—the undifferentiated origin of all things, Japanese—no longer in general use, except at Ise Shrine where it has been used since ancient times on flags signifying Amaterasu Ōmikami); the concept of *daiwa* (meaning a state of ideal peace, but in Japan used to refer to Yamato, the center of the country); and the Taoist concept of immortality. Early Japanese perhaps regarded their ceremonies and beliefs as Taoist, even though they may have differed from those in China. Hence, it is possible to view these teachings, rituals, and even the concepts of imperial authority and of nation as remnants of an attempt to establish a Taoist tradition in Japan. If that is so, Japan's ancient popular beliefs were not so much an indigenous religion but merely a local brand of Taoism, and the word Shintō simply meant Taoism. The accepted theory today is that a systematic form of Taoism did not enter Japan in ancient times, but it is not unreasonable to think that over a long period of time Taoism gradually pervaded Japan's religious milieu until medieval times when Buddhism dominated it completely.

Three possible interpretations of the word Shintō in the *Nihon shoki* have been presented above. It is not yet possible to say which of these is correct, but that should not preclude certain conclusions about Shintō. What is common to all three is that none views Japan's ancient popular beliefs as an independent religion and none uses the word Shintō as a specific term for such a religion. Also, there is no evidence that any other specific term existed. Moreover, when Buddhism was introduced into Japan there was a controversy over whether or not to accept it, but there is no indication that these popular beliefs were extolled as an indigenous tradition. Hence, Shintō need not imply a formal religion per se, and it need not indicate something that is uniquely Japanese . . .

[Editor's Note: In the next three sections, omitted here, Kuroda Toshio examines the institutional importance of the kami in the ancient period, the meaning of the word *Shinto* in the medieval period, and Shinto's secular role during the same period. He points out that during medieval times the word *Shinto* generally meant "kami" and was understood to be a part of Buddhism. Hence, Shinto was thought of as just another form by which the Buddha teaches and saves humans. Often the kami were depicted in secular roles such as nobleman, Chinese gentlemen, hunters, ladies of the court, and travelers. They were called upon in all kinds of secular settings (before battle, to witness an oath, for good fortune in business) while the Buddha was more often called upon to secure a good rebirth or peace in the "next world."]

THE EMERGENCE OF THE CONCEPT OF SHINTŌ AS AN INDIGENOUS RELIGION

The following two sentences are found in the *Shintōshū*:

1. Question: On what basis do we know that Shintō reveres the Buddha's teachings?

2. Question: How are we to understand the statement that the Buddha's realm and Shintō differ in their respective forms but are one and the same in essence?

Both of these questions pose kami and Buddha against one another. In the first Shintō clearly indicates the kami themselves, whereas in the second Shintō may be interpreted as the deeds, state, or authority of the kami, but it also conveys the idea of a realm of the kami by contrasting it to the Buddha's realm. A similar passage is found in the *Daijingū sankeiki* by Tsūkai:

> Amaterasu Ōmikami is paramount in Shintō and the Tathāgata Dainichi is paramount in Buddhist teachings. Hence in both *suijaku* (manifestation) and *honji* (origin or source) there is the supreme and the incomparable.

In this case Shintō may be understood as the ideal state of being a kami, but it is also important that, as a concept juxtaposed to "Buddhist teachings," it assumes a sphere of its own, meaning "the realm of *suijaku*," teaching and converting in the form of a kami. This is especially true of the Ise school's theory of Shintō. For example, in the *Hōki hongi* Shintō is contrasted to the "three jewels" (the three basic components of Buddhism—the Buddha, the Buddhist teachings, and the Buddhist order), or in the *Ruishū jingi hongen* it is juxtaposed to *bukke* (Buddhist schools). These imply that Shintō and Buddhism belong to separate spheres in the phenomenal world even though they are identical in essence. Examples that transfer emphasis to the word Shintō in this way are quite conspicuous in Ise Shintō. This was a natural tendency, since the Ise school's theory of Shintō had to stress the efficacy of Shintō above all, even more than other schools of sectarian Shintō.

The word Shintō, when set up as an object of contrast in this way, emerged with a sectarian meaning or with a special sphere of its own, even though fundamentally it meant the authority of the kami or the condition of being a kami. This is not to say that it immediately assumed the meaning of a separate teaching or religion liberated from the framework of Buddhism. Rather, what Ise Shintō tried to do was to cast the realm of Shintō in a resplendent light. This was attempted by reducing the terms contrasted with Shintō to purely Buddhist phenomena and forms—namely, Buddhist teachings, "three jewels," Buddhist schools, and so forth—and by defining Shintō relative to them. All the while, Buddhism, the overarching principle that embraced and unified both, was left intact as the ultimate basis. The Ise school also attempted to aggrandize Shintō by diverse embellishments and additions to Shintō that were non-Buddhist and by cloaking it in a dignity similar to that of the Buddhist scriptures. Nonetheless, in this case also the principles that Shintō held in common with Buddhism were likewise stressed.

In this way the word Shintō came to refer to a Japanese phenomenon, school, or sphere of Buddhism qua religious truth. This meaning of the word paved the way for later stages in which Shintō became a term for Japan's indigenous religion. The writings of the priests at Ise as well as the theories of fourteenth-century Shintō thinkers such as Kitabatake Chikafusa, Jihen, and Ichijō Kanera (corresponding to Tsuda's third definition of Shintō, "concepts and teachings concerning kami") played a particularly important role in this process. Nevertheless, it was not because these thinkers were critical of *kenmitsu* Buddhism, which was the orthodox religion of the medieval period. Rather, they were all adherents of the orthodox teachings, so that any statements they made, which might at first seem to oppose those teachings, were nothing more than an attempt, extreme though it may have been, to enshroud in mystery the authority of the governing system at a time when it was isolated and in decline. With the rise of the Shintō-only school (Yuiitsu or Yoshida Shintō) at the end of the fifteenth century, the word Shintō became more and more identified as an indigenous form of religion. It was even interpreted as the highest religion, though identical in essence with Buddhism and Confucianism. At this point the meaning of the word began to depart from the orthodox teachings of *kenmitsu* Buddhism. It just so happened that during this period the power of the orthodox religious order was in a state of decline because of the strength of various heretical movements of so-called new Buddhism, particularly of Shinshū uprisings (*ikkō ikki*). The Shintō-only school, which was one branch of sectarian Shintō, simply took advantage of this situation for its own unfettered development.

Beginning in the seventeenth century a Confucian theory of Shintō, with much the same structure as medieval theories, was formulated by Hayashi Razan and other Edo period scholars. Based on this interpretation of Shintō, the definition of Shintō as the indigenous religion of Japan, as opposed to Taoism, Buddhism, or Confucianism, became firmly fixed. Moreover, the Confucian concept of *dō*, the way, also influenced the word Shintō, imbuing it with the meaning of "the way, as a political or moral norm" (Tsuda's fifth definition of Shintō). Of course, Confucian Shintō amounted to nothing more than theories of the educated class subordinating Shintō's true nature to Confucianism. Actual belief in the kami, however, as found among the common people at that time, remained subsumed under Buddhism.

The notion of Shintō as Japan's indigenous religion finally emerged complete both in name and in fact with the rise of modern nationalism, which evolved from the National Learning school of Motoori Norinaga and the Restoration Shintō movement of the Edo period down to the establishment of State Shintō in the Meiji period. The Meiji separation of Shintō and Buddhism (*shinbutsu bunri*) and its concomitant suppression of Buddhism (*haibutsu kishaku*) were coercive and destructive "correctives" pressed forward by the hand of government. With them Shintō achieved for the first time the status of an independent religion, distorted though it was. During this period the "historical consciousness" of an indigenous religion called Shintō, existing in Japan since ancient times, clearly took shape for the first time. This has remained the basis for defining the word Shintō down to the present. Scholars have yielded to this use of the word, and the population at large has been educated in this vein.

There is one further thing that should be pointed out. That is that separating Shintō from Buddhism cut Shintō off from the highest level of religious philosophy achieved by the Japanese up to that time and inevitably, moreover artificially, gave it the features of a primitive religion. Hence, while acquiring independence, Shintō declined to the state of a religion that disavowed being a religion.

CONCLUSION

This article is an attempt to trace Shintō throughout Japan's entire religious history by extracting samples dealing only with Shintō from each period. The reader may be left with the impression, contrary to the assertion at the beginning of this essay, that Shintō has indeed existed without interruption throughout Japanese history. This is only natural considering the sampling method used. Moreover, it is undeniable that there is a certain continuity to it all. Therein lies the problem. Up to now all studies of Shintō history have emphasized this continuity by means of such a sampling process. In doing so they have applied to all periods of history a sort of surgical separation of Shintō from Buddhism and thus from Japanese religion as a whole. By such reasoning, anything other than Shintō becomes simply a superficial overlay, a passing thing.

The meanings of the word Shintō, as well as changes over time in customs and beliefs, would indicate that Shintō emerged as an independent religion only in modern times, and then only as a result of political policy. If that is so, can this continuity be regarded as a true picture of history? Or could it be that what is perceived as indigenous, or as existing continuously from earliest times, is nothing more than a ghost image produced by a word linking together unrelated phenomenon? Up to just one hundred years ago, what constituted the religion and thought of the Japanese people in most periods of history was something historical—that is, something assimilated or formulated or fabricated by the people, whether it was native or foreign in origin. This thing was something truly indigenous. In concrete terms, this was the *kenmitsu* Buddhist system including its components, such as Shintō and the yin-yang tradition, and its various branches, both reformist and heretical. It, rather than Shintō, was the comprehensive,

unified, and self-defined system of religious thought produced by Japan in premodern times. Even today it is perpetuated latently in everyday conventions as the subconscious of the Japanese people.

Throughout East Asia, Mahāyāna Buddhism generally embraced native beliefs in a loose manner, without harsh repression and without absorbing them to the point of obliteration. The question here is how Japan should be interpreted. While acknowledging Japan as an example of this East Asian pattern, should one consider the separation of Shintō and Buddhism to be an inevitable development and, in line with Meiji nationalism, perceive Shintō as the basis of Japan's cultural history? Or should one view *kenmitsu* Buddhism's unique system of thought, which evolved historically from diverse elements, including foreign ones, as the distinguishing feature of Japanese culture?

Considering the magnitude of the problem, this article leaves much to be desired. It is hoped, however, that it has served to dispel fictitious notions about Japan's religious history and religious consciousness, and about Japanese culture in general.

9

Women and Shinto

From a modern egalitarian perspective, women have not faired well when it comes to organized religion. They have been denied roles of leadership, their interests have been subordinated to male interests, and they have been generally treated as second-class citizens. Shinto is no exception in its subordination of women.

This treatment of women under Shinto may be somewhat surprising because Shinto's Sun Goddess Amaterasu is the primary kami of the land. Also, both male and female energies play important roles in the creation myths. In addition, women were once priestesses and served as mediums, communicating the will of the kami to people. Further, women played an important role in healing and, as we saw in the case of Tenrikyo, sometimes were founders of new religious movements.

Okano Haruko explores the issues surrounding women and sexism in Shinto in the following selection. She argues, among other things, that various factors played a role in the decline of the influence of women within the Shinto tradition.

OKANO HARUKO

Women and Sexism in Shinto

READING QUESTIONS

1. What is the twofold task of this article?
2. What three factors are responsible for the decline of priestesses?

Okano Haruko, "Women and Sexism in Shinto," *The Japan Christian Review* 59 (1993): 27–31. Reprinted by permission of the author.

3. What is the situation like today with regard to women and Shinto?
4. What is the principle of Japanese society that sustains Shinto?
5. What is the significance of this principle in a global society?
6. How does Amaterasu "hide Japanese sexism"?

The task of this article is twofold. The first is to trace the change in the position, meaning, and role of women in Shinto, and the second is to consider critically how Shinto participated in the formation of women's image and arrived at a sexist stance. I shall show this by reconsidering the meaning and role of women in Japanese society as developed by Shinto. My first aim is to delineate Shinto's progressive disownment of women's spiritual power which had been acknowledged by the ancient Japanese, of women's exclusion from the center of religious life, and of the gradual deprivation of women's autonomy. My second is to show how the issue of feminism in an undifferentiated, unitary society is different from Western societies where a person is established as an individual.

In modern Japanese society, Shinto coexists with an advanced technological economy. This is a peculiar phenomenon as Shinto, which is very alive, still maintains its archaic animistic beliefs and ancestor worship. Shinto's perdurance demonstrates the persistence of the spirit of the Japanese who locate themselves in the original life-community which developed naturally. The ancient Japanese were convinced that their communal well-being was guaranteed by the gods. Within ethnically grouped communities, individual members do not differentiate between themselves or between themselves and the world around them. Consequently, those who display individuality in Japanese society are not easily accepted, while those who go with the stream are welcomed.

WOMEN IN THE HISTORY OF SHINTO

Shinto, the "Way of the Gods," so-called to distinguish it from *Butsudō* the "Way of Buddha," is a collective term for several different forms of religion. Besides primitive Shinto, there are Shrine Shinto, the orthodox form which includes Imperial Household Shinto; popular Shinto, the religion of the people; and finally Sect Shinto, a set of independent systems. I will not include Sect Shinto here, which I consider to be akin to the New Religions, because its content differs qualitatively from the primary form of Shinto. Thus, excluding Sect Shinto, Shinto can be classified historically into three periods:

1. Primitive Shinto, from early history to the organization of Shinto, from the end of the 2nd to 7th century CE.

2. Organized Shinto, from the Taika Reform to the Meiji Restoration, 645-1867.

3. Shinto after the Meiji Restoration, 1868 to the present day.

It is not quite certain whether in Japan's early history, the existence of priestesses preceded that of the priests or not. We cannot say whether a golden age of women ever existed or not. The actual state of Shinto in its early period has not been sufficiently clarified. A much more important problem is the relationship between men and women in that period where this can be historically substantiated. In the earliest stages, rulership implied priesthood, and as the social structures included both men and women, so too power in the ruling classes was distributed between men and women in rather interesting ways. The woman was the medium of direct contact with the deity and announced the divine will to humankind. The realization of this will on earth was entrusted to the man. Thus priesthood was embodied in a male plus female relationship, usually brother and sister. This system is found first in the clan systems (*uji*), then in territorial administrations of the provinces (*kuni*), and in the centralized government of the Yamato Empire.

However, in time this man plus woman system underwent changes. The more dependent everyday life was on the mystical, magical elements in religion, the more important was the woman's role. Proof of this is that many of the *miko* (female shamans) were deified and the ancient chronicles speak of female rulers such as Himiko and priestesses such as Tamayori-hime. However, as the rights and privileges of the various petty rulers were gradually absorbed by the Imperial family and a centralized empire formed, politics assumed an increasingly rational character, although it was supposed to be determined ultimately by divine will. Thus began the formal and conceptual rift between politics and religion, as a result of which women retired more and more from this form of society, for example, in the case of cult princess Saio. At this stage the woman was only the emperor's representative in the religious sphere, and the same process could be observed in the independent provinces.

The second period of Shinto history began with the Taika Reform which brought about a change from the old form of government to a centralized absolute monarchy. In order to achieve political unity in the state, the power of the earlier provincial lords fell to the emperor. This meant that the individual cults of the local gods of the clans (*ujigami*) had to be organized into one central system. Thus such local deities, originally worshipped only by certain clans, took on an official and national character. The Department of Shinto Affairs (*Jingikan*) was set up to organize religious life and to see to the administration of the shrines. In this sense the religious cult had now become the rationalized concern of the bureaucrats instead of being the spontaneous act of a naturally religious person. In former times individuals endowed with charism had summoned the gods and these had taken possession of certain chosen persons. But in State Shinto, fulfilling the rite correctly meant that the gods could only appear at a certain time and in a certain place. For this reason, the rites had to be performed by official priests, and the bureaucrats of the Jingikan, sometimes assisted by other court dignitaries, male or female, officiated at ceremonies in the shrines at the Imperial court and at other shrines of major importance, while the rites at local shrines were the responsibility of the provincial governors (the *kokushi*) and priests such as the *kannushi*, *negi* and *hafuri*. These official priests were as a rule men, but in many old shrines the tradition of having a priestess persisted until the tenth century CE. After this time priestesses were very rare, but at Ise, the Imperial ancestral shrine, the body of priests was led by a priestess up until the Middle Ages.

Three factors are responsible for the decline in the number of priestesses at most shrines: 1) since the descent of the divinity could now be calculated "mechanically," as it were, women were no longer really necessary in the priesthood; 2) the Chinese legal system, recently introduced to Japan and on which the priesthood was based, was strictly male-oriented; and, 3) Buddhism strengthened the notion of the uncleanness of woman, due to her biological and psychological make-up.

The newly created bureaucratic state took over the religious rites and the priesthood and organized them, thus rendering them static; but charismatic figures, mostly women, continued to be active among the people, outside the system of organized Shinto. We may find them in secularized types such as dancers, puppeteers or courtesans, or even as pillars of popular Shinto, the belief of the people.

Each new step in the modernization of the cultural, political or economic fields ousted women further from significant positions in the priesthood, because their religious authority, often inherited, was based on the supposedly superstitious religious notions among the people.

The third period, beginning with the Meiji Restoration, also considerably affected the position of women. The newly restored Imperial dynasty, with its new national awareness, strove to establish pure Shinto as the national religion, and abolished such mystical elements of Shinto as the concept of inherited charism and also the practice of magical rites. Women could no longer be a member of the official priesthood.

Since the Second World War, however, women have once again been accepted into the priesthood. No distinction is made between them and their male colleagues and both men and women fulfill the same functions. It must be admitted, though, that women are generally seen as substitutes for male priests. Thus women have achieved a new position in the Shinto religion by renouncing their specific femininity, which was the source of their traditional function and role within the religious community.

At present, there are about one thousand Shinto priestesses in Japan and equality of the sexes is progressively being pursued. However, there remain two problems from a feminist perspective.

1. The participation of women is limited at the higher ranking shrines, such as Ise and Atsuta, which had prerogatives during the period of National Shinto.

2. Shinto is still sensitive to contamination by "impure blood," so that priestesses have to take precautions so as not to defile the cult during menstruation. Their menstrual periods are controlled and regulated through the use of medications.

While the traditional functions of women within organized religion may have all but vanished, the miko, female sorcerers, are once again active among the people. They will tell fortunes and prophesy, for a consideration, and also function as medicine women. The great number of female founders of sects should also be mentioned. Their new teachings on religion and values and their faith healing claims appeal to the mass of the people. Religious communities founded by such women existed even before the Meiji dynasty. This particular type of charismatic women see themselves as mediators between gods and people, and filled with prophetic awareness, as foundresses of universal religious communities. This is a new phenomenon in Japanese religious history, but it is interesting to note that such "new" religions show in their community life old elements of primitive magic and base their authority on the tradition of the "classical" religions.[1]

SHINTO AS THE CAUSE OF JAPANESE SEXISM

Shinto, the original indigenous religion of Japan, survives even to this day and lies at the basis of Japanese industrialized society. In this section I shall consider the following two points: what is the principle of Japanese society which sustains Shinto, and what is the significance of this principle within the global society. As I mentioned above, Shintoistic society is pervaded by an ethnic religion and a life community spirit. Within such community, therefore, the individual member has a comfortable view of religion based on the conviction that good fortune and well-being are guaranteed as long as the individual remains within the community which is protected by the deity. Individual Japanese maintain the sense of a unitary society without differentiating from one another or from the world. In Europe, Christianity in the process of the civilization of the Latin and Germanic societies, abandoned the blood-relational clan community and the old group consciousness of nondifferentiation. At the same time in Arabia, Islam replaced its primitive ethnic religion. In India also, although it occurred during a short period of its history, Buddhism awakened to the concept of the individual and replaced the varied forms of ethnic religion which had previously responded to the spiritual needs of the community.

In Japan, imported foreign religions such as Buddhism, Confucianism, Taoism, and even Christianity could not dismantle the Shintoistic unitary community spirit. On the contrary, the Shintoistic community enforced a sense of familial solidarity by means of the extended family. Moreover, by placing the emperor at the top of society and regarding him as divinely descended, Shinto affirmed the absolute and sacred nature of the nation, while Buddhism and Confucianism assisted in the formation of this ideology by underlining its authenticity. The characteristics of the Japanese unitary society as a pseudo-national community is understood in terms of an all-embracing maternal principle, according to Kawai Hayao.[2] Westerners divided society dualistically into sacred and profane, good and evil, superior and inferior, and as a result suppressed the weaker elements in society, while the Japanese glorified the equality of the members of their society sustained by the family principle which embraces everyone indiscriminately. In this sense modern Japanese capitalism is the offshoot of Japanese Shintoistic state ideology. As long as one stays within the social order undergirded by this maternal principle, peace and prosperity are guaranteed, just as children are embraced equally at the bosom of their mothers. Thus, Japan grew to be a civilized nation where basic education spread to the remotest area without laying financial burdens on the people.

Looking back on the history of Japan, there are not a few who attempted to cut off such maternal bonds and who tried to assume autonomy. But within Japanese society, one generally finds it difficult to take up the issue of individuality or distinctive personality. On the contrary, it is a condition for survival not to be too different from others. A man who desires to be a person with individuality experiences strong resistance from society similar to the efforts required of a woman trying to overcome assigned roles. Moreover, Japanese consider that everything in the world is built on relationships. This is underlined by Confucian moral theology which postulates five human relationships and cardinal virtues. Within these relationships, everyone, man and woman, superior and inferior, is expected to sacrifice oneself. Consequently, this has resulted in creating a general feeling of victimization. From a woman's point of view this psychic structure makes it difficult to objectify sexism. It is evident that no person among the more than one hundred and twenty million Japanese can remain a child at the mother's breast. Hence, the ultimate task of Japanese feminism is an anthropological issue of how each individual can establish his or her own identity.

In spite of Shinto's maternal principle which operated within Japanese society, the formation of public order and institution of the national community was in the hands of the male with an androcentric frame of mind as I described above. It is my opinion that the thrust for such patriarchalization of Japanese society sprang from the political will to power of the imperial family who promoted this centralization. The source of power of the imperial family is the divine authority derived from the ancestral deity, Amaterasu, as the *Kojiki* and *Nihongi* describe. Since Amaterasu is the ancestral goddess of the Imperial family, the Sun Goddess who governs the universe and who occupies the highest position in the Shinto pantheon, she serves to hide Japanese sexism. It is similar to the Christian cult of the Blessed Virgin Mary which is deeply involved with the issue of sexism.

Amaterasu, who was originally the mother of the god of the rice plant, a priestess who played a simple role, was raised to the state of noble virgin goddess thereby proving the sacredness of the imperial family. This was a creation by those who held control of the value system within patriarchal power. This is akin to the process of the glorification of Mary, the raising of the simple mother of Jesus first to the status of eternal virgin and mother, and then to the final glory of assumption into heaven.

The reason why Shinto can sustain meaning in Japan today can be found in the coexistence of the formal side of the androcentric national cult with the ethnic religion represented by woman in the background. Moreover, for the sake of the spiritual peace of the community, Shinto allowed both god and Buddha to survive together within it, thus strengthening its own authority in the community.

As Japan underwent the processes of modernization, religion was deeply involved in the formation of its ideology: Shinto and Buddhism were utilized to achieve centralization and form legal institutions; Confucianism was used in the establishment of the feudal system in the modern period; and Shinto repeatedly played a decisive role in the Meiji restoration. Outwardly, the religions had no role to play in the rebirth of Japan from defeat in war to the democratic state it is today, except for the period immediately after defeat. However, religion always justified the central institutions and the familial system. Inwardly, Shinto maintained its strong hold on the Japanese people, justifying and supporting sexism and class discrimination, and reinforcing fascism.

Shinto belief deified those who died a heroic death. Thus it exalted the soldiers who died in the "Holy War" of Japan as deities. Hence, both men and women were compelled to interiorize the meaning of serving their country. One of the important causes of the immaturity of the Japanese with regard to autonomy and independence lies in their consciousness of the national and familial community which is peculiar to Japan. Shinto, together with Buddhism and Confucianism which were accepted by Japan, should be criticized and indicted from the feminist perspective, since they fermented, reinforced, and justified this understanding.

NOTES

1. For a detailed account of women's position and roles in the history of Shinto, please refer to my *Die Stellung der Frau im Shinto* (Harrassowitz, 1976), p. 19ff.
2. Kawai Hayao, *Bosei shakai Nihon no byōri* (Chuōkōronsha, 1976).

Appendix

PRONUNCIATION GUIDE

In Japanese, vowels are generally pronounced as in English as follows:

a as in *father;*
i as in *image;*
u as in *rude;*
e as in *late*, and when final is usually short as in *end;*
o as in *roster.*

Each vowel is one syllable, hence it is pronounced separately. So *Saiin* (title for the imperial princess priestess at Kamo) is pronounced *sa-i-i-n*. Also, Japanese has "double vowels" which are pronounced longer. Therefore, *soto* is *so-o-to-o* not *so-to*.

Consonants in Japanese also generally follow English pronunciation with the following exceptions:

n can be a syllable by itself and is pronounced like *n* in *pen;*

double consonants are pronounced with a staccato so *tt* sounds like *cattail* and *kk* is pronounced as if separated by a hyphen *k-k; g* is pronounced like an English *g* except when it appears in the body of a word and is then often pronounced *ng*.

In addition,

tsu sounds like *ts*, as in *its*, with the addition of the Japanese *u*; and *chi* sounds like *che* as in *cheese* and *cho* sounds like *cho* as in *chocolate*.

KEY TERMS AND CONCEPTS

Amaterasu The Sun Goddess and imperial ancestor.
Domestic Shinto Practices centering around the home altar and principally concerned with family ancestors.
Folk Shinto A popular form of Shinto largely practiced among the rural population.
Imperial Household Shinto This refers to the rites conducted at the three shrines within the palace grounds.
Izanagi This male kami along with his female counterpart, Izanami, created the islands of Japan.
Izanami The female kami who is the cocreator with Izanagi of Japan.
Kami This term can refer to a variety of sacred objects, including gods, spirits, ghosts, trees, mountains, ancestors, and superior humans, such as heroes.
Kamikaze Divine winds thought to protect Japan.
Kojiki *Records of Ancient Matters* dating from 712 and containing stories about the creation of Japan, the generations of kami, and the early emperors.
Nihongi *Chronicles of Japan* dating from 720 and containing ancient myths, legends, and early history of Japan to 697.
Sect Shinto Thirteen officially recognized religious movements that did not receive support from public funds during the Meiji Restoration.
Shrine Shinto Ritual practices conducted at the thousands of shrines dedicated to kami and found throughout Japan.
State Shinto A version of Shinto supported by tax dollars and declared by the government during the Meiji Restoration not to be a religion, but a set of traditional cultural values and practices.
Susanoo The wind kami and younger brother of Amaterasu who rules the sea.
Three imperial regalia The mirror, the sword, and the curved jewel, all of which have mythological significance and are in the possession of the reigning emperor as a sign of imperial power, authority, and divine descent.
Tsukiyomi The moon kami who rules the night and is the younger brother of Amaterasu.

SUGGESTIONS FOR FURTHER READING

Bellah, Robert. *Tokugawa Religion: The Values of Pre-Industrial Japan*. Glencoe, IL. The Free Press, 1957. A classic sociological study of Tokugawa Shinto, in which the author probes the question, "Was there a functional analogue to the Protestant ethic in Japanese religion?"

Earhart, H. Byron, ed. *Religion in the Japanese Experience: Sources and Interpretations*. Belmont, CA: Wadsworth Publishing, 1997. An excellent collection of source material relating to Japanese religions arranged topically.

Kitagawa, Joseph. *Religion in Japanese History*. New York: Columbia University Press, 1966. The most comprehensive historical study of Japanese religion in English.

Nelson, John K. *A Year in the Life of a Shinto Shrine*. Seattle, WA: University of Washington Press, 1996. This study provides detailed information on what goes on in a Shinto shrine during a one-year cycle.

Ono, Sokyo. *Shinto: The Kami Way*. Rutland, VT: Charles E. Tuttle, 1962. This book provides a brief overview of Shinto by a former professor at Kokugakuin University, which is closely connected to the Association of Shinto Shrines. It has apologetic undertones but provides a good example of Shinto's self-understanding today and valuable information from a well-educated insider's point of view.

Ooms, Emily Groszos. *Women and Millenarian Protest in Meiji Japan*. Ithaca, NY: Cornell University, 1993. A study of the roles women played in developing the new religions of Japan.

Reader, Ian. *Religion in Contemporary Japan*. Honolulu, HI: University of Hawaii Press, 1991. This book focuses on religion "at the ground level" and seeks to provide an account of the ways in which religious themes find their way into the lives of the Japanese people.

Yuso, Michiko. *Japanese Religious Traditions*. Upper Saddle River, NJ: Prentice Hall, 2002. A concise

and accurate introduction to Shinto for the beginning student.

RESEARCH PROJECTS

1. Write a comparative study of wedding ceremonies in Shinto and some other religion of your choice.
2. Conduct a Web search for information about Shintoism and write a report describing and evaluating some of the resources you find.
3. Put together a comparative analysis of the different theories developed in Japan to characterize the relationship between Shintoism and Buddhism.

RELIGION ON THE WEB: SHINTO

http://www.wfu.edu/organizations/ssjr
This is the Web site of the Society for the Study of Japanese Religions maintained by Jay Ford. It contains many useful links as well as a wealth of information by reliable scholars.

http://www.religioustolerance.org/shinto.htm
General information about Shinto at a site maintained by the Ontario Consultants on Religious Tolerance, whose goal it is to promote the right of people to hold religious beliefs "without hindrance or oppression."

http://www.sacred-texts.com/shi
This site presents a variety of texts and older studies relating to Shinto, including translations of excerpts from the *Kojiki* and *Nohongi* dating from the late nineteenth century.

http://www.tenrikyo.org.jp
This is Tenrikyo's Web site. Like most of the new religions of Japan, Tenrikyo maintains a Web site to promote the organization's beliefs and practices.